INTRODUCTION

A few years ago a very interesting thing happened to me when a woman approached me and offered me a photograph which showed me, in my punk days, sniffing glue in one of the subways which were situated at what is now Custom House Square. Now at the start of our conversation I thought that she was offering me this as a gesture but what it turned out to be was she was trying to blackmail me to get money. I was described at the time as "Belfast's most prominent local historian who had written extensively on the subject" and what this person was doing was offering to sell me the photograph so that it would never fall into the public domain. Now I must admit I was curious to see the said picture as I wanted to see who I was with and what we were up to. What happened was that when I found out what she was up to I told her where to put the said photograph which involved Vaseline and a very dark place in the human anatomy. What she didn't bank on was the fact that I do not deny my past and that I quite openly talk about it. So here I am now being described as 'Belfast's most important historian' but I would be the first to state that it was not always this way. When I thought about it I remember the photograph being taken. It was of us leaving Paddy Rea's bar where McHugh's is now situated. We were making our way to a concert in what was called the Anarchy Centre in Lower North Street to watch Poison Girls who were a very well known punk band of the time. Now there's no doubt that the said lady is going to be reading this and all I would state is for her to get her facts right. We were NOT sniffing glue – we were sniffing black rubber solution!

This book is not designed to make me money, in fact the profits are going to charity (The Joe Baker International Travel and Drinking Foundation – joke, joke!) Its purpose is to show kids whom society has given up on that all is not lost. I was given up on from an early age and when I left school I could hardly read or write. Yet when I realised the time was right I self educated myself and have now gone on to do better than many who spent years studying hard in university. Five thousand copies of this book are going to be printed and my aim is to simply to get through to one unfortunate kid whom society has lost all hope in. My message to him or her is simple. Someday you are going to realise that you are going to have to make something of your life and get on with it. Because of your mistakes you will think that this is going to be impossible but you take my word for it – if I can do it then so can you. I hope that this book will show how I did it and that it will be an inspiration for you to do it too. My message to you is this. If there is something that you want to be or want to do then there is only one thing stopping you and that is YOU! As Goethe once stated "Whatever you can do, or dream you can do it, begin it."

When you are ready then just go for it and remember one thing. You did not fail society – society failed you!

As for the woman who tried to blackmail me with the glue sniffing photograph its just a pity you did not give it to me. It would have made one hell of a front cover.

ANCESTRY

They say that to know yourself then you need to know where you came from. Well if this is the case then I would have to say that I would seem to know myself pretty well.

I had always grew up hearing different stories about my grandfather, Rabbie Baker, who was extremely well known the in York Street area. He had lived in an area known then as the Fenian Gut which was bordered by York Street, Henry Street, North Queen Street and Great George's Street. Today there are many who argue that it stretched as far as Lancaster Street but with the area long gone and most of its original residents now dead I guess that today we can only speculate.

Martin Lynch, the Belfast playwright's, grandmother was my grandfathers sister and during research for a play Martin traced the Baker family back to the Shankill Road area with my great grandfather being Protestant. The story went that my grandfather was also a Protestant but in the 1911 Census of Ireland he is listed as Roman Catholic providing us with another strange mystery. The head of the house is listed as my grandfather's older brother Samuel with them all living at number 8 Columbus Street. Samuel at the time is aged 18 but where were the parents? Now I know that they must have been around somewhere because Martin's grandmother is not listed on the Census return and through the returns no trace of her or her parents can be found. It would seem that my great grandfather was indeed a Protestant from the Shankill Road area and that he

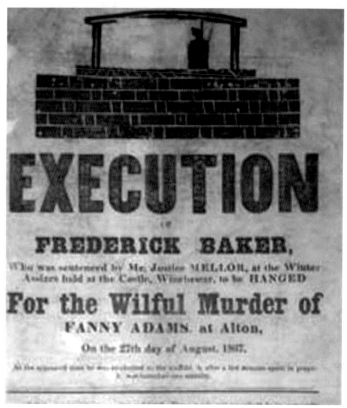

either had a religious conversion or that he married a Catholic and that the children were brought up in that faith. Sometime ago another member of my family, on my mother's side, had been working on his family tree. Because my mum's dad was different to her sisters and brother due to her mum's remarriage he decided to look back at the Baker connection. He too traced it back to the Shankill area and also to the fact that we came

1911 Census of Ireland Form for 8 Columbus Street.   My grandfather is at no. 4

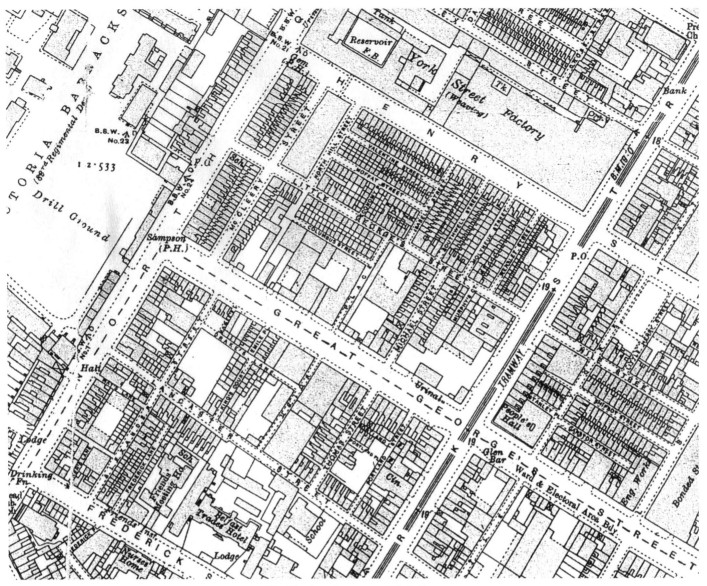

The Fenian Gut area of York Street

from England in the 1860's (well I always figured that as the name was a bit of a give-away!) Anyway his findings led to something a little bit more sinister. Apparently (or should that be allegedly) our family came to Belfast in the late 1860's from Hampshire but what could be sinister about that?

No doubt many of us have heard the saying Sweet F A but believe it or not it does not mean the obvious. What it actually means is Sweet Fanny Adams as this was a poor little girl who was murdered and cut up so badly that there was very little left of her hence the saying. Now here's the real sinister bit. Fanny Adams was murdered by a man named Frederick Baker in Alton, Hampshire in 1867!

Changing the subject quickly we'll get back to the 1911 Census Return (left) and to the then head of the household Samuel Baker. He was also well known in the area through his talent for swimming and it is said that if tragedy had not struck he would have become a champion. However tragedy did strike a few years later in the 1920's and while swimming Sam took severe cramps and drowned.

It was also around this time that the partition of Ireland took place and the bloody civil war which broke out in Belfast. In this area shootings and bombings were a daily occurrence and in the immediate area atrocities such as the Weaver Street bombing and McMahon Murders occurred. The bomb attack in Weaver Street was against a group of Catholic children playing in the street killing a number of them and the McMahon attack occurred in March 1922 when a gang led by high ranking members of the R.I.C. burst into a Catholic home and shot dead all the male members in the front room.

The McMahon Family a subject I later studied and wrote about

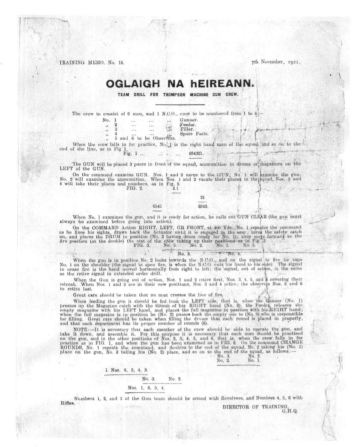

One of the IRA documents Rabbie Baker was caught with

Rabbie Baker (left) in the Irish Army.
To the right is Paddy Kearney

But the atrocities were not just all one sided and another nearby attack was carried out against Protestant workers in a cooperage in Little Patrick Street when gunmen walked in, lined them up, and shot them dead. Over the years I had heard stories that my grandfather had been involved in this but to my relief I later discovered that he had been in prison at the time. He had been caught in possession of IRA documents and with having a B-Specials warrant card. He also had a nicked vice the purpose of which is unknown but even I would conclude that it was for no good. He was sentenced to the Belfast Prison on the Crumlin Road and looking at his release forms there is an interesting note at the bottom of them which states that upon his release he was to have been interned. This never happened as he was released and fled across the border and joined the Irish Army.

The Belfast Prison on the Crumlin Road
Three generations of the Baker's were here for a while!

How this occurred is another family mystery but one of the stories is that he was told of the threat of internment by his uncle who was a warder and who was married to his aunt and who in turn was one of the Baker's from the Shankill.

He remained in the Irish Army for some time and when it was safe to do so he returned to Belfast. It was at this time that he married a woman named Suzie Bradley from Ballymacarrett and all my aunts, uncles and of course dad came along. It was also the time coming up to the thirties when my grandfather was to be at it again. This time he set up an armed group known as the Catholic Defenders Association in the area of the Fenian Gut. The stories have it that he was in charge of Sailortown but this is untrue as the group was led there by a man named Barney Boswell. However he was in charge of the York Street area and this time it did include the Lancaster Street district. The purpose of this group was defence and there are numerous stories where Rabbie Baker did indeed open fire on people attacking the area mainly during Orange parades. This earned him the nickname 'Peter The Painter' due to the type of gun he used. Peter The Painter was Peter Piaktow, a Latvian revolutionary, who had escaped a siege in London's Sydney Street and who had used a German Mauser C96

and which went on to become known as a Peter the Painter. (Above) This gun was extremely reliable and could have a butt attached to it and was the gun only used by Rabbie Baker. The R.U.C. knew he had it but could never find it even though they raided his house after every gun attack. In his house Rabbie Baker had a section dug out on the chimney breast in a bedroom which was covered by an altar. It was behind this that the gun was always enclosed. In the early 1930's the R.U.C. had organised a raid in a local club known as Glenravel which was enclosed behind houses in North Queen Street with open ground to the front and side of it and where Rabbie Baker had been giving a lecture on its use. At this place was an old iron works known as The Piggy and loud noises where the norm. They found the butt of the gun but not the gun itself. It is said that the gun was smuggled out by being concealed in the bra of a local woman and because it had been fired during training it is said that the gun burned her and left a nasty scar on the woman's breast. Once again this is a local myth but the fact remains that the gun was never found and Rabbie Baker was charged with having the butt. Needless to say because

the gun butt was found in a public establishment there was no proof that it was actually in his possession. He "beat the rap," as they say but then came another interesting stage of his life. It is said that he had wanted to go and fight for the International Brigade during the Spanish Civil War. This would sound about right as he greatly admired the leader of the Soviet Union of the time, Josef Stalin. Now looking at someone whom was determined to do his bit for the international cause then you would imagine that one would need a real good excuse for not being able to do so. Well what was Rabbie Baker's excuse? His wife wouldn't let him! So it is true. Behind every great man is a great woman.

Rabbie Baker was a committed communist and greatly admired the then leader of the Soviet Union, Josef Stalin

It would seem that after this Rabbie Baker settled down and although a committed communist he never got involved again in local politics. He earned his living by using his hands and in his back yard in Moffat Street he had a basic workshop where he could mend almost anything. Martin Lynch remembers playing out in this yard and remembers his bench with all the tools of the trade including a large vice – something I get the feeling that he didn't exactly pick up in McMaster's! Rabbie Baker died in 1962 of a heart attack at his Moffat Street home. His funeral did not go into the local chapel (St Patrick's on Donegall Street) and stories went that this was because he was actually Protestant. It had nothing to do with being Catholic or Protestant but was because of his communist beliefs.

RAID ON CLUB BY POLICE AND TROOPS. July 18 1935

Court Sequels to Riots—Twenty-four Detained Men Released.

A combined raid by police and military upon the Glenravel Club in North Queen Street was described during the hearing of further riot cases at Belfast Custody Court yesterday.

The police are still making arrests in connection with the disturbances on the nights of the 12th and 13th in the York Street area, and two more men were remanded on charges of unlawful assembly and riot.

It is understood that the 24 men who were detained following the attack upon the "International Bar" in Donegall Street on Tuesday have been released. No charges were preferred against them.

Mr. H. H. Mussen, Crown Solicitor, prosecuted.

A raid by police and military upon a club in North Queen Street resulted in the appearance of Robert Baker, Moffett Street, charged with being unlawfully in possession of firearms on June 16. Mr. G. Magee defended.

Constable Taylor said that shortly after 11 o'clock on the morning of July 16 he went to a club known as the Glenravel Club in North Queen Street, where he saw a number of men, and searched them. Baker came out of a door behind the club, and as soon as he saw the constable he rushed back into an adjoining room. A lance-corporal of the Border Regiment who was with witness caught the accused.

When he charged Baker with having firearms he denied possession. Witness added that the butt of the gun (produced) had been handed to him by the lance-corporal.

Cross-examined, witness said that Baker told him he was the caretaker of the club that week. The club was frequented by hundreds of men.

The man was remanded in custody for a week.

RUSHED POLICE CORDON.

Two Men Shot and Houses Wrecked.

James Watson, Valentine Street, was charged with riotous assembly on the night of Saturday last.

Sergeant Swindell said that while on duty in Nelson Street, Whitla Street, and Marine Street he saw a crowd of people numbering about 300 shouting, "Look at him," referring to a man who had been assaulted. He heard defendant shout, "Rush them," and "Come on, boys," referring to the Nationalist crowd in Marine Street and North Thomas Street.

A police cordon had been drawn across North Thomas Street, but the cordon was broken by the crowd, who proceeded to wreck a number of houses. Two men were shot and a number of persons wounded as the result of the riot.

He arrested Watson that morning at 26, Trafalgar Street. When cautioned he said, "I have nothing to say."

Asked by the Clerk if he had any questions to ask, the accused replied in the negative, adding that the sergeant was "telling a lot of lies."

Glenravel F.C. in the mid 1920's. Rabbie Baker is seated second from the left on the front row

And so ended the life of one on Belfast's characters and my only regret is that I never knew him as I wasn't even born yet. But when I look back I really do think that there is an element of truth to family instinct. Allow me to explain. For years I was a brilliant swimmer and won all sorts of badges, medals and trophies for doing it. I literally took to it like a duck to water and even today, after thirty years of smoking, I am still a very good swimmer with a preference to wild rivers and the sea – just like Sam Baker. For some reason I am extremely good with DIY and this ranges from electrical work right through to gardening. The only thing I get stuck with is plumbing. Have a guess what Rabbie Baker was useless at!

There's also the political element. I have no shame in stating that I am a communist – something that Rabbie Baker was extremely well known for. This is something that you can argue was passed from generation to generation but my dad had never any interest in politics so where did this develop from?

They do say that you can pick your friends but you can never pick your family but to be honest I don't care – with such a wonderful history I wouldn't have it any other way.

Rabbie Baker (front third from left) with the North Hill Darts Team in 1950

Rabbie Baker (second from right) with the Darts Team in 1950. These photographs were taken in McGurk's Bar on North Queen Street which was to become infamous after a no warning Loyalist bomb attack some years later

MY FAMILY

Reading the previous chapter you could be forgiven for thinking that I know everything there is to know about the Baker side of things but this is untrue. Like a lot of families I seemed to have grown up mainly on my mum's side of the clan knowing very little of my dad's side. I think this was all because my dad was, in the old fashioned way of things, the provider and was therefore always working. Family visits were therefore always made to my mum's mum and sisters. I have distance memories of my grandmother but as for my mum's sisters I do remember almost every visit. Granny had been married a few times and mum's dad was different to that of her older brother and sisters. Her dad was called Joe Duffy and he worked for the White Star Line (owners of the Titanic) and was in the Merchant Navy. His ship was torpedoed by a German U-Boat in the Irish Sea in 1940 and he was killed. My mum had two sisters, Kathleen and Suzie and a brother Willie. Uncle Willie left Belfast shortly after the Second World War and joined the R.A.F. where he spent the next thirty five years. Serving in all the troubles spots during the 1950's and 60's he met his wife while posted to R.A.F. Leeming in Yorkshire.

Granny Greer (mum's mum) with cousins Michael, Stephen and Robert Greer around 1967

but it was more to do with where she lived. Out the back of her house was a river which ran down past the back of the Falls Park and down under the Glen Road. I had a fascination with rivers and coming from the concrete jungle where I lived rivers and open spaces were new to me.

As a child I can remember going to stay in my Aunt Kathleen's and my brother Liam staying at my Aunt Suzie's in nearby Norglen Road. I can only guess that when we stayed here it was because of problems my Mum and Dad were going through of which I'll talk about later. Needless to say I always enjoyed staying at Aunt Kathleen's because of the green space and rivers but also because she had a large back garden and Uncle Davy loved his gardening and showed me stuff he had planted and grown himself. What's interesting is that in future years when I brought my own son David up he loved my uncle Davy and his gardening and it was only through this that I realised that it was indeed the same interest and fascination that I had had grown up with all those years before. These were basic interests and were interests which stuck with me for life. I can remember my Uncle Davy showing me a small helicopter type seed and he told me that this would grow into a massive tree and do you know to this day I have a fascination with trees and with growing them. Today when I travel abroad in the Autumn I always pick various seeds of trees and you would be surprised at the amount of trees from places as diverse as Moscow and Berlin that are now growing in North Belfast and all this being possible from Uncle Davy's explanation of how trees grow!

As I said the Falls Park was at the back of my Aunt Kathleen's house and at that section of the park was an outdoor swimming pool known as the Coolers. We had many visits to this but I could never work out why as it really did live up to its name and was absolutely freezing – all year round!

Uncle Willie who left Belfast to join the R.A.F.

There were four children in the family, Uncle Willie, Aunt Suzie, Aunt Kathleen and of course my mum who was the youngest. Although the youngest my mum was the first to die followed by Aunt Kathleen. Aunt Kathleen and Aunt Suzie lived in Turf Lodge and as a child I remember going to stay in their houses. We all have favourites and mine was my Aunt Kathleen

At times we also stayed in Aunt Suzie's house but I don't remember staying in her house in Turf Lodge. Before this she lived in a big house on the Springfield

FAT

temperamental and surprise shows in his choir-boy face. "I'm not temperamental," he says, "I'm just impulsive."

Now he prefers not to talk of the past. he'll say conclusively to anyone who tries to discuss it with him.

Born Alfredo Arnold Cocozza, in a poor Italian district of America. 35 years ago. Mario claims that even as a child he knew he was going to become famous.

...ing lazy as a boy, his only hobby was collecting Caruso records. While other boys were out playing in the streets, Mario would stay at home playing the records over and over. When he was only seven years old he played ... record 27 times at one sit... he had a ... accompanied a Caruso ... found he could reach notes of a particularly ...ce.

...ided to be a singer, ... practical grandfather ...ed that he ... al work. So ... a job moving

...occasion he ...lp move a ... concert hall ... famous con-...was due to ...er the job ...hed Mario ...resist mak-...afters ring ...voice. The ...heard the ...ted to see ...came from.

and then took Mario under his wing.

After Mario sang in Hollywood he was given a film test—it his looks did not help him. When he'd slimmed and had his complexion toned down with pink powder, he was given another test. This was successful and he started to make films.

Immediately fans were crazy

LANZA LINES

He is 5ft. 11in. tall, but wears built-up shoes because he thinks his width makes him look deceptively short.

He ... 59in. chest and ... he sings in the bath he gets dizzy from wall vibrations.

He has now a wardrobe of opera clothes for possible future use. He bought all the operatic costumes he wore in "Serenade."

He eats on his own when he's dieting, because he can't bear to see other people "making pigs of themselves."

with the charm and fire that have long made lovers of the Latins. After four films his temperament caused his studio some worry.

But now back at work again. the temperament in Mario seems to have vanished. "I want to devote my working life to my singing, and my private life to my family," he says.

Home to Mario is a mansion, and his family comprises his wife and four children. "I am in love with each and every one of them," he says. Another member of the family is a St. Bernard dog that Mario bought because he was such a cute little thing. Today the dog is even Mario over.

By Hollywood standards the Lanza house is considered large. It has a great marble hall and a cinema that seats 80 people. There are six bathrooms and seven television sets. Mario's bed is ten feet wide and eight feet long and cost £600.

"WONDERFUL — I could have slept through it twice!"

200 highlights

HAPPY ANNIVERSARY! the latest idea in congratulations by music, starts to-night's broadcasting from Radio Luxembourg (208 metres) at seven o'clock—and heralds another weekend of star listening to the stars. Here are the highlights.

TO-NIGHT: 7.30—Lamir Gold and his Pieces of

Eight; 8—Friday's Requests; 8.30 — Forces Favourites; 9—Handful of Stars; 9.30—Oh!; 10—Masters of Melody; 10.30—Record Hop; 11.30—21 Record Show.

TO-MORROW: 7.30—Irish Requests; 8—Jamboree; 10—Scottish Requests; 10 ... Club; ... Round-up.

a skilled job, a fine future and now... higher pay

Here's sweet music for all film fans. This signed picture of a tenor can be your for only 6d. Mario Lanza, the golden-voiced Bros. star, would be a notable addition to your ... Also still available are pictures of Frank and Fess Parker. See coupon (below) for ... how to get them.

Please send me a photograph of:
MARIO LANZA   FRANK SINATRA   FESS PARKER

Name.................................

Address...............................

....

Now more than ever, the Royal Air Force is a job worth thinking about. Here are three good reasons why.

Higher pay (since April 1st). The new R.A.F. pay rates look pretty good alongside the wages for similar jobs in civilian life. **Skilled training** If you're between 17½ and 40, the R.A.F. offers one of the finest technical trainings in the world. **Money to spend** Most of your new, bigger R.A.F. pay packet stays in your pocket; food, accommodation, clothing allowance are all free—and you get 30 days' leave each year on full pay. Here's a secure, well-paid job with promotion assured for the able man.

22 trade groups include: aircraft, radio, armament, electrical and instrument engineering — general engineering — air traffic control — radar operating — photography — medical — dental — secretarial — catering — police — music — R.A.F. Regiment.

HOW YOU COULD GET AHEAD IN THE R.A.F.

At 21: Junior Technician earning £7.17.6 a week, all found
At 24: Corporal Technician (married) earning £13.4.10 a week.
At 34: Chief Technician earning £17.8.10 a week.

A skilled career at higher pay in the R.A.F!

Post this today! TO: ROYAL AIR FORCE (R.V.227), VICTORY HOUSE, LONDON, W.C.2. Please send particulars on training for skilled trades in the R.A.F., including full details of increased pay, promotion, leave, pensions, etc.

NAME....................................

ADDRESS................................

_____ Date of Birth _____   (Applicants from British Isles only)

At one time Uncle Willie became the 'face' of the R.A.F. - that's him in this newspaper advertisement dated 8th June 1956

Me and mum at 10 Downing Street, London

Dad and Liam outside Buckingham Palace, London

Kathleen Neeson, Suzie O'Reilly and Jean Baker (mum with sisters)

Christie Baker, Charlie Baker (dad) and Seamie Baker

Mum

Dad

The 'Coolers' at the back of the Fall's Park which, take my word for it, really were cool in the true sense of the word!

Road and with that big house came a big garden. I have to say that I absolutely loved that big garden and my early memories again revolve around trees as out her back she had an orchard of both apple and pear trees. Once again there was an interest in trees but also of what could grow on them. I was never really an apple person but loved pears and the harder they were the better and to this day I still love hard pears a taste of which seem to have evolved from my Aunt Suzie's wild garden on the Springfield Road.

It is strange where you develop a taste for things from. Another example is my love of blackberries. Now my earliest memories of these are from visits to the doctors. I have no idea why but my mum's doctor was a Dr McKee who was based in Short Strand. When we had to go there either for me or mum then it was certainly not a matter of phoning the nearest taxi depot – it was walk over and walk back again. I enjoyed the walk over because it took us along the Laganbank Road and there, at the rear of the Oxford Street Bus Station, grew a massive blackberry bush. I can state that I must have picked every berry from this bush dozens of times and to this day still have a love for them – preferably wild.

Oxford Street Bus Station had a massive blackberry bush growing wild at its back and I can state that I must have picked them dozens of times. Just like McGurk's Bar previously mentioned this bus station was to become well known after a horrific bomb attack a few years later.

Now looking at my interest and love of wild fruit you could be forgiven for thinking that childhood influence could be nothing to do with all this and that it is all just an acquired taste. As I mentioned Aunt Suzie had both apple and pear trees out her back and my love was for the pears. Well on one occasion Aunt Suzie's son George was messing about and threw an apple off the tree and it whacked me right in the eye. Needless to say I ran crying to Aunt Suzie and was told to stop whinging and to dry my eyes but its strange that to this day I love every wild fruit but still have a hatred of wild apples.

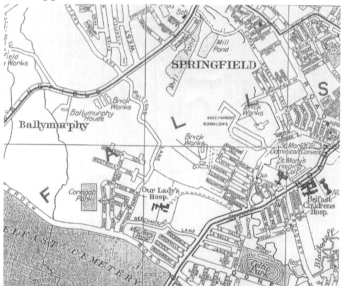

The Flush

Another set of memories I have of visiting there was that at the front of her house was an area known as The Flush and once again it had a river running through it and once again I was fascinated with it. We must have spent hours playing there and to one side of it was a large scrap yard. I remember this well as we constantly played here in and out of all the scrap cars. I had two favourites here. One was an old crane and the other was an old excavator and the items which I loved about these was their caterpillar tracks and I have always had a fascination with how they worked and to this day I love watching them in operation and the bigger the better. I should have stated that I had three loves in this old scrap yard as the other thing I was drawn to was the old Morris Minor cars. Today I have no interest in cars or with driving but over the years I have built up a large collection of items relating to Morris Minors ranging from scale models right through to repair manuals and log books. Now tell me that that interest did not begin playing in this old scrap yard!

The river was also a source of adventure and it was here that I remember all of us catching spricks and frogs. What we did was get old jars and nets and spend hours catching them but why I will never know as all we did with them was let them go afterwards. There was also another past time spent here on similar lines and that was catching wasps and bees. Sounds dangerous and

Photograph of the Sailortown area in 1960's. To the right (No.1) is a small section of the Fenian Gut area and at the bottom (No. 2) is the site of the soon to be constructed Artillery Flats

I'm sure looking back it was. The idea here was to get a milk bottle and watch for wasps and bees landing on a flower. We would then place the opening of the bottle over the flower and therefore catch the said stinging insect and then place a bit of netting over the opening. Once again you could ask why but it kept us occupied for hours and kept us outdoors

This was all my mum's side of the family and as already stated I knew very little on my dad's side. Of course I know all my aunt's and uncles but know very few of my cousins but quite often I am mixed up for being them. For example one of my dad's brothers settled in the Sailortown area and two of his sons were named Liam and Joe. Now me and my brother Liam are mixed up all the time. Sadly Liam (cousin) died on the 7th of August 2008 and the amount of people that approached me and stated that they were sorry to hear about my brother were countless. Liam (cousin) was a well known IRA prisoner in England and was convicted for trying to blow up the Queen's boat the QE2

There is no doubt that my dad's side of the family are the biggest and not only includes the Baker's but also the White's in the New Lodge, the Lawlor's in Short Strand and various branches stretching from Liverpool

Liam Baker (cousin)

to London. What I find unfortunate is that I know so few of them and I could walk past a lot of them in the street and not know any of them. An example of this was at my dad's funeral as I could state that of all the people there I knew about a third of them.

ME, MYSELF AND I

And so it comes to me. I arrived on this planet on the second hour of the second day of the second month in the year 1965. Now for anyone thinking "great" I have his name and date of birth so its time to apply for all sorts of credit cards don't bother wasting your time. I can't even get anything through Ocean Finance so my credit must be really bad!

Although I am well known for being from the Barrack area of the New Lodge I was not born there. I was born at 67a Ormeau Road which was a small flat facing the Gas Works. Needless to say I have absolutely no memories of living there or of the places we moved to soon after. Mum and dad moved to a flat above a bicycle shop on Duncairn Gardens and then to a place

My mum Jean

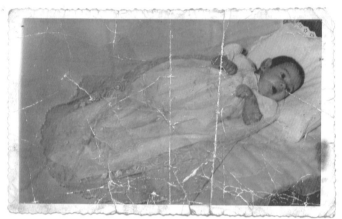

Christening of Joseph Baker, March 1965, at St. Malachy's Chapel

My dad Charlie (left)

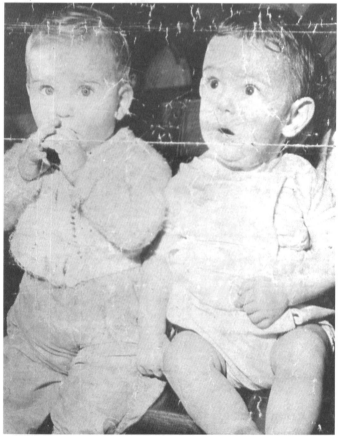

The first ever newspaper picture of yours truly from 1965. The caption read as follows:- Eight-months Heather Telford (left) Ormeau Street, and eight-months Joseph Baker, 61a Ormeau Road, soon became friends when they met at the clinic.

in Atlantic Avenue in the Newington area just off the Antrim Road. From there they moved into a flat on the fifth floor of the newly built Artillery Flats on North Queen Street which was built on the site of the old Victoria Barracks complex.

Soon after dad got a job as a caretaker in another of the recently constructed flats called Churchill House, a flat in which our family has remained until this very day. One of my early memories is moving from Artillery Flats to Churchill and at that time I was only four or five. Because dad was the caretaker we had the ground floor flat at the entrance and I always remember him getting up at 5am to start his work. I knew this because I helped the milkman and soon after and had to get up at 6am. When I say I helped the milkman that is exactly what it was as I was unpaid but the joy I got riding around in the milk float was pay enough for me.

Photograph of big brother Liam taken on his second birthday in 1962

Mum and dad with Liam and cousin Mary O'Reilly (left)

From left to right Edward (Chubby) White, cousin, Mary O'Reilly (cousin), Liam Baker and Danny Lawlor (cousin)

Mum and dad were Jean Duffy and Charlie Baker. They were married in St Peter's in the lower Falls in 1960 shortly before my older brother Liam was born. After Liam came their second son called Charles but sadly he died. I was not around at this time but the circumstances surrounding him break my heart as I know it must have gutted mum and dad. My aunts (mum's side) have told us that he was buried in Milltown Cemetery and that they had to do the whole thing themselves. Today I cant help but think how heartbreaking that must have been. I was the third child and third son and the memory of my second brother lives on in me as mum and dad decided to name me Joseph Charles. Charles the father and Charles the son.

Churchill House was a tower block which was built right in the heart of the Victoria Barracks complex.

Photograph taken from St Patrick's spire of the tower blocks around 1967. At the front is Churchill House and to its left is the remaining section of Victoria Barracks which is now the Carlisle Estate

When we moved in there was still a section of the Victoria Barracks facing our flat and this was used by the T.A. before they moved into the nearby Girdwood Park. This section of the Barrack was demolished and work began on what was to become the Carlisle Estate. I remember as a child playing here and on one occasion I can remember going home with no shoes on my feet. Mum had asked where were my shoes and my reply was that I had got them dirty and put them into the big washing machine to clean them. Needless to say the big washing machine was a cement mixer and someone within Carlisle Estate has my shoes underneath their floor! Looking back I actually think that these are amazing memories as they are actually before I started primary school but moving on to that subject primary school is really where the memories begin!

St Patrick's Primary School

Talking to people over the years I seem to be the only person who seems to remember their first day at school. I can remember the actual room, teacher, being left at the door, and bloody crying my eyes out. The school in question was St Patrick's Primary School on North Queen Street but if memory serves me right I think its actual address was on Lancaster Street. The school is now gone and so is my first classroom but the first teacher was Mrs Hunter. Now this was her mar name and she went on to become principle of S

Photograph taken in 1962 from one of the tower blocks looking towards the city centre. To the centre right can be seen part of St Patrick's Primary School. The building in the foreground with the tower is The Recy where we spent most of our time. The building directly behind the tower is McGurk's Bar.

the Sea but I remember getting left at the classroom door and Mrs Hunter giving me Lego to play with. What happened after that is a blank and like everyone else I only remember the basics. The basics for years afterwards for me was getting up around 6am and helping the milkman, returning home to collect schoolbag and then making my way to school. In those days St Patrick's had no uniform so there was no getting changed but my fondest memories were of the lollipop man on North Queen Street facing the top of Lancaster Street. He was always friendly and knew the names of every single kid from the area. I always looked up to him and dreamed of being him but although I can remember his face, coat and of course lollipop I could never remember his name but Billy is my instinct. Another unique thing about the school was the boys and girls being kept apart with one section for each sex. I can remember playing in the main ground and how teachers stood in the centre to make sure we stayed apart - now how stupid was that!

At the top of Lancaster Street was Lizzie Loughran's shop and this was always the first port of call before

school. This was a real old fashioned shop and when you went in there were newspapers etc. laid out on the right hand side and sweets etc. on the left so you don't have to be Einstein to work out where we went. The people who owned it we obviously called Loughran and my memories were that they were very, very old. Looking back I can only imagine that they must have run this shop for something to do because I seem to remember that it was always open and they talked to everyone that came in including us kids and seemed to have their own names for everyone. For example Mr Loughran always referred to me as 'Joe 90' after the popular Thunderbirds type character of the time.

My main memories of the school were the constant bomb scares. I remember countless occasions when we were all taken out and and brought up to the football pitch in the Barrack area which was directly facing the school and being counted. One bomb attack I do remember was actually next door to the school when, in December 1971, McGurk's Bar was blown up killing fifteen people. This happened on a Saturday night but I can remember all the children gathering at

McGurk's Bar

McGurk's Bar the day after the no warning loyalist bomb attack. Our tower block, Churchill House, is in the background

The funerals of some of the victims of the McGurk's bombing leaving our estate.

the site on their way along North Queen Street. I was one of them and although I can remember the actual bomb and knew that there was people killed I can not remember a single funeral. At a guess I assume that all the children must have been kept well away from the back playground, which was on North Queen Street itself, when the funerals were passing.

At my time in the school the headmaster was Mr Johnston and the main teacher I had was Mr McKee. For the last few years in the school my classroom was one of the outside huts. Although the school was built to accommodate 400 boys and 400 girls for most of the 1970's additional huts had to be erected in the front

and back playgrounds to keep up with demand. Our hut was the one at the top of Lancaster Street and in winter they were great. In the school building the classrooms had high ceilings and massive windows, but the huts - small windows, low ceiling and electric radiators - what more could you want. The downside however was that if it was a sunny day you were toasted.

I can remember almost everyone I was in this class with and looking back I am delighted that I was in with such a unique and diverse bunch. Most of us were broke up going into secondary school but fortunately all my friends with the exception of one ended up in the same class when we started 'Barny' a few years later.

Needless to say there are thousands of stories centred around this classroom but the one I remember the most was when one of the boys came in with a massive bundle of money and gave it to the teacher. '"Here sir," he said, "that will do the monopoly game." He had picked up this wad of money in Lancaster Street and handed it over to the teacher thinking that it was toy money. The teacher handed it in to the peeler barrack on North Queen Street and the owner was discovered but what the story was behind it I still don't know.

On the Lancaster Street side of the school were many of the old run down Victorian houses which were eventually demolished. In one of them I remember the Gallagher's had an old wood cutting concern where sticks were cut for fire wood. I assume that is what it was but if I'm wrong - sorry Philip! Behind the Gallagher's concern was a waste paper or scrap yard or both. Behind this was a caravan site for travellers and on the Great George's Street side was another site. I think some of these children went to the school at one time or another but none were in our class. We would all like to live in an equal world but they say that kids are the cruellest and our relationships with these children was far from perfect to say the least. However, our relationship with the kids who went to St Malachy's Primary School at the bottom of the New Lodge Road was no bundle of laughs either.

On the Great George's Street side of the school was a scrap yard which was always filled with old cars. Can you imagine what sort of a play ground this was to us kids! Beside this was the old Rocktown Bar and it was here that us kids had our first taste of beer. A wooden crate of bottles was accidentally left outside one day when we were getting out of school. Needless to say it somehow ended up in our hands. After working out how to get the pressed caps off we had our first sip of the hard stuff - and it was bleeding stinking!

As mentioned I started school at the beginning of what became known as The Troubles so not knowing it then my education was going to be one hell of an experience. On our school days once we got our breakfast into us it was out of the pyjamas, washed, clothes on and off to school. Now observant readers will note that I made no mention of a uniform and the reason for that is quite simple - we didn't have one. I have no idea why this was but the only reason I can think off is our parents simply couldn't afford it but regardless of the reasons I didn't care because if there was one thing I hated, it was a school uniform. Once we were out the door we never seemed to be in a hurry to get to our classrooms. I remember then that one of our favourite past times was watching the troops at the nearby peeler (police) barrack through the gaps in the security fencing. The place was packed out with jeeps, saracens and various other military vehicles so as very young children you can see how these fascinated us. On a few occasions we even managed to get in so here we had one of the most secure cop shops in the whole world having their security breached by a few kids on their way to school!

Once we got to the school it was into the playground for a bit of messing about before role call. St Patrick's at that time was split into a boys section and girls section and when we were in the playground we were never allowed near each other which I found pretty weird considering we would more than likely be with them after school anyway. We were then lined up outside to see who was in and then paraded of to our classrooms. Now I don't mind admitting it but I really hated school with a passion and I can tell you it was one place I never wanted to be but that was life and we

When we went to primary school bombs were exploding in Belfast left, right and centre and were used, by us, to secure days off. This one was just down the street from our school in York Street.

had to grin and bear it. Mitching school then was a bad idea because of the Troubles but when we found a good excuse then it was used to our full advantage. I remember one time going to school and there was a bomb scare over in Clifton Street. I went back home and told my mum that there was a bomb scare near the school and secured a day off. Now North Queen Street was not sealed off but I did not lie to my mum as Clifton Street was indeed near my school. The following morning I secured a note from my mum mentioning that she kept me off for the day due to the bomb scare - result. Now in those days bombs were going off left, right and centre so this excuse could be used time and time again. Sadly, like every scam, the teachers caught on and that was the end of that.

Just as we were never in any hurry to get to school the same applied going home. I can honestly state that at primary school I can never remember doing any homework. That's not to say we didn't get any, I just don't remember a single incident of actually doing it (maybe it was them bomb scares again!) On our way home we would have gone to a friends house either in the New Lodge, Sailortown, Half Bap or Unity Flats. We would have sussed out each other's toy collection and in those day there were only two toys you dared have. The first were what were called 'midges' which were inch high toy soldiers and the second were Action Men. Now these were real Action Men and not the stupid looking things they make now. Any other sort of plaything was instantly dismissed. If we were not playing with these then it was outside for a game of Hingo, Two Man Hunt, Kick the Tin or our version of Cowboys and Indians - Brits and Rioters. Brits and Rioters was a simple game, when you saw soldiers you threw stones at them or pretended to be Provies and shoot them with our improvised guns which were nothing more than a bit of wood. This was proof of how life around us was having a massive impact on our way of thinking because we had absolutely no idea who the Brits were, who the Provies were and what the hell was going on. All we saw was the excitement and we wanted to incorporate that into our playtime.

Although there was a massive dinner hall in the school I can honestly state that I was only in this a few times as I always went home for my dinner. The advantage here was that I could sit down and watch the mid afternoon kids programmes on TV which then consisted of my favourite Pimpkins and Hartly Hare - words fail to describe how much I loved him as he was the most cheeky, sarcastic thing on TV. Pimpkins was followed by Rainbow and my favourite character here was Zippy who just happened to be cheeky, sarcastic etc., etc., so at least now you know where I got it all from! It was also around this time that I became aware that my mum was not like all the others. It's very

Our version of Cowboys and Indians was Brits and Rioters. This photograph from 1974 was taken on the site of the McGurk's Bar bombing at the junction of Great George's Street and North Queen Street.

difficult for me to explain but I remember mum drinking stuff called Mundies and then going all funny. I could never understand why but I was soon to learn and learn very, very quickly. Mum was an alcoholic but you need to understand that at this time I didn't even know what drink was never mind what it could do to you.

At times when I went home I had to lift mum from the floor after she had drank a considerable bit of Mundies Wine. The norm for me was putting her to bed, making sure she was comfortable, pouring out most of what remained of her wine and replacing it with water. I would then have went and made myself either a tomato sauce sandwich or, if my luck was in, a Sugarpuff sandwich and then settle down to my programmes and then back to primary school for the afternoon session. Needless to say when I got home mum would have still been in bed and I would then tidy up the flat and peel potatoes for dinner as that was all I could do. As time went on I learned to do different bits and eventually I could prepare and cook a whole dinner and have the flat cleaned for dad coming in from work as mum lay drunk.

Needless to say I thought that this was just happening to me but through the years I was to discover that a lot of my friends and other kids throughout the district had alcoholic parents and I'm sure that many of them went through the same thing as me or even worse where violence was involved. Don't get me wrong this was not constant and only occurred when mum hit the drink and although these are difficult memories I must state that most of my childhood memories of mum are indeed happy ones.

Happy ones until I describe how mum dressed me. Now for those not in the know allow me to explain where I lived. The Barrack area of the New Lodge was easily one of the toughest inner city working class areas there was. Add to this the fact that there was a war going on between the IRA and the British and the fact that there were patrols of the latter every single day. Now that you have a mental image of the area try and imagine the survival rate of a kid running about in shorts, a shirt and a tie all spotlessly clean. I would love to be able to say that I was describing another kid in the district but I'm afraid that its me! Don't ask me why but my mum

I would love to say the kid on the left is me but I'm afraid not as that is Joe Mowbray. I'm the other in this 1971 photograph.

must've thought she lived somewhere completely different as this was what I was sent out in for the first few years of my life.

I think the last time I wore shorts was at my 1st Holy Communion in May 1972. I can remember getting ready for this and mum pulling out white shorts, white shirt and a bright red tie and some sort of medal I had to wear. I had had enough of shorts but she had told me that all the other kids had to wear them as it was part of the religious thingy. On going into the chapel have a quick guess who was the only person wearing shorts and have a guess who was the only person who got slapped about later! I can remember this day like it was yesterday and can state that I hated every second of it.

This is me on my Communion day with mum and brother Liam who seems to be enjoying every minute! Could I ask that the fact that I am being held down for this photograph be taken into consideration!

Like all good Catholics I remember going around all my relatives on my First Communion and getting dosh. I then remember my mum going to the women's section of Lynch's Bar (a boxed off area with separate entrance) at the top of the New Lodge Road. It was around this time that I would've played with Carolyn Stewart as my mum would send me out with her. Why my mum sent me out to play with a girl was totally beyond me but with me in my shorts at least I had someone weaker than me. The names I called that girl where unbelievable and if she grew up hating me I can honestly state that I don't blame her. Sometimes we played in North Queen Street and there was a sweetie shop nearby and in those days Walnut Whips were sold out of a tray instead of the wrappers they come in today - they were also twice the bleeding size! These always seemed to end up in our pockets but Carolyn never seemed to get the actual walnut as this was my favourite and I nicked hers off the chocolate before handing over her share.

Carolyn and I used to explore everywhere and our favourite was the old derelict houses behind the Diamond Bar in Hardinge Street and many an hour was spent hoking through each one. At this time I would've been around 7 or 8 but I think Carolyn was younger than me. On another occasion we were together in the old local graveyard and we would have gone around looking at all the old headstones reading them. Although not realising at the time this is where my interest in local history was to begin but I was saying nothing at the time as history was not the sort of subject you bragged about.

Hardinge Street looking down towards North Queen Street

OUR CASTLE IN THE SKY

I remember reading somewhere that the friends you develop in childhood are the friends you have for life. I can associate with that because although I have a lot of friends from all walks of life those from childhood are my closest and most trusted.

When we moved into Churchill House you need to understand that this was everyone living more as a community than as neighbours. For example today we hear of all the funded reports which state of the horrific condiditions children have to put up with through high rise living. All I would say is get your funders to look at case histories such as us. It never done us any harm and I can actually remember bringing people from school into my flat to show them an indoor bath. If they thought that was amazing then you should've seen their faces when they saw hot water coming out of a tap! Most of these kids lived in the long streets of the New Lodge and their toilet was outside. For a proper wash they either had to wait in line for the tin bath or go to the public baths which we today call swimming pools.

The friends I developed in the flats in childhood really are my true and most trusted friends today. Churchill House was twelve stories high and therefore, including ground floor, consisted of fifty houses. Now if I were to list all my friends from this block alone then it would take sometime but I will highlight the most signifiant as they will be mentioned elsewhere in this publication. I understrand that to the reader this may appear boring but you need to understand that it is very important to me so I will start from the top to the bottom.

At number 12 three of my closest friends lived. Scelf, Jamesy and Jim. Scelf was Scelf O'Neill (12c), Jamesy was Jamesy Davidson (12b) and Jim was Jim Madden (12a). Many an hour was spent with all of us sitting at the washhouse, twelve stories up, looking out and wondering what would happen if the Russian's launched an attack. Our playtime consisted of Action Men and what we called 'midgies' which were the tiny toy soldiers of the time. We also had 'big soldiers' which were slightly bigger and 'little big man' which was a

Churchill House in 1971 (bottom). Our flat was on the ground floor to the left

66 Laing, Mrs. Phyllis
68 Creighton, Mrs. M. N.
70 Shannon, J.
72 Hoey, J. H., engineer
74 Occupied
76 Aspley, Arthur J., manufacturers' agent
78 Connor, Wm. J., clerk
80 Madden, James C.
82 Connolly, Denis, publican
84 Alexander, Samuel L.
86 Cuthbertson, Dorothy
88 Greer, James, coach builder
90 Sheppard, Albert, lry drvr

VICTORIA PARADE

At 60b North Queen Street
New Lodge, E. Belfast (U.K.);
New Lodge (N.I.)

ALEXANDER HOUSE
Code BT15 2EP

Flats—

G1 Croughwell, Mrs. Kathleen
G2 Higgins, Mrs. Mary
Flats—
1a Warnick, Thomas
1b Quigley, Mrs. Joan
1c O'Neill, Mrs. Jane
1d McKenna, T., foreman
2a Kelly, Charles
2b Smyth, James, docker
2c Davis, Gerard
2d Service, Wm., electrn
3a Friel, Daniel
3b McCabe, John, lorry drvr
3c Smith, S. J., steward
3d Deaghan, Mrs. Elizabeth
4a Farmer, Mrs. Mary
4b Cullen, Edward
4c Monaghan, Mrs. Mary Jane
4d McGeown, Felix
5a Hughes, R., labourer
5b Wylie, Thomas
5c Gallagher, M., lorry drvr
5d Loughrey, Miss M., textile worker
6a McGreevy, Mrs. M., usherette
6b Jacobson, Mrs. Bridget
6c Magennis, Francis
6d Lundy, A.
7a McAlea, John
7b McNulty, Trevor
7c Loughran, David
7d O'Neill, Terence, docker
8a Quinn, T., labourer
8b Quinn, James
8c McBride, William, fitter
8d McAlister, H., electrn
9a Bailey, John
9b Hughes, Patrick, hodsman
9c Loughrey, T., electrn
9d Crelan, Richard
10a McWilliams, John
10b Faulkner, D., electrn
10c Adams, George
10d Hamill, P., docker
11a Quinn, Mrs. Mary A.
11b McDonnell, James
11c Nolan, Francis
11d Murphy, Brian
12a McAloney, William
12b Maitland, Daniel
12c Whitson, James
12d Cox, James

2-64 Code BT15 2EN
2 Burns, Hugh, docker
4 Hennessey, Mrs. Martha
6 Largey, Patrick, docker
8 Brown, Francis J., barman
10 Marley, Mrs. Jean
12 Davey, Bernard
14 Gillen, Mrs. Catherine
16 Duffy, Mrs. Catherine
18 McLeish, Mrs. Margaret
20 Loughlan, Terence, upholstr.
...Here is Queen's Parade..
22 Nolan, John, painter
24 Tosh, Mrs. C.
26 Molloy, Thomas, clerk
28 Barnes, Joseph, hall steward

30 Megran, Mrs. Mary
32 Flanagan, Mrs. Margaret
34 Austin, P., labourer
36 Donnelly, R. T., manager
38 Irvine, J., P.O. official
40 Hamilton, James, helper
42 Black, Miss Isobel
44 Crangle, Mrs. E., coil wndr
46 Doherty, B., redleader
48 M'Donald, H., driver
50 M'Anulty, John, ganger
52 Loughran, Mrs. Annie
54 Henry, Mrs. Elizabeth
56 O'Hagan, Mary I.
58 Cassidy, Mrs. Ellen
60 M'Ateer, W. J., irondresser
62 Steele, P., pipecoverer
64 M'Cotter, Wm., bricklayer
82 Donnelly, Mrs. Martha
84 McGreevy, Henry
86 Fogarty, Mrs. Mary
88 Darling, Mrs. Bridget
90 McCann, Mrs. Elizabeth

CHURCHILL HOUSE
Code BT15 2EQ

Flats—

G1 Baker, C., caretaker
G2 McCullough, John, watchman
1a Robinson, H., linesman
1b Miskimmon, Mrs. Mary
1c Donohoe, Mrs. Mary
1d Donnelly, Mrs. Mary
2a Croughan, James, dckr.
2b Austin, R.
2c Kerr, Miss Clara, cook
2d Connor, Joseph, driver
3a Brady, John
3b Spallen, Gerald, clerk
3c Devine, Mrs. Catherine
3d O'Boyle, Patrick, commissionaire
4a Gowdy, Mrs. Katherene
4b Downey, Miss Rose, waitress
4c Roche, Miss Sarah
4d Brennan, Miss Josephine
5a Tiegan, John
5b Kelly, James
5c Smyth, Joseph, monumental worker
5d O'Neill, Charles, docker
6a Darragh, Alfred, painter
6b O'Neill, James P., dckr
6c Duff, Thomas, labourer
6d McCartney, Bernard
7a Aylward, Martin
7b Morgan, James
7c Ludlow, C.
7d Tohill, T., barman
8a Fields, John, driver
8b Digney, Alexander
8c Moore, B., clerk
8d Maione, Robert
9a McAnally, D.
9b Woods, —
9c Donaghy, G., painter
9d Magee, George, bus dvr.
10a Lillis, John
10b Hillis, J.
10c McIlroy, James
10d McBride, Charles
11a Shepherd, Albert, lorry driver
11b Thompson, Mrs. Rose
11c Brady, Henry
11d Connor, John
12a Madden, Joseph, lorry helper
12b Davidson, Samuel, labr.
12c O'Neill, M., labourer
12d O'Neill, William

VICTORIA ROAD

From 62 Palmerston Road to Inverary Drive
Sydenham, E. Belfast (U.K.);
Sydenham (N.I.)

Side door
Gateway

1-53 Code BT4 1QU
1 Hoey, Terence, mechne
3 Donnelly, Andrew
5 Boucher, W., lorry dvr.
7 Martin, Mrs. Martha
9 Lamb, David A., joiner

11 M'Clelland, Archibald, joiner
13 Morton, William, pipecoverer
15 Frazer, Stanley, fitter
17 Vacant
19 Faulkner, Mrs. Rose
21 Johnston, D.
23 Paul, James, fitter's hlpr
25 Greenaway, Mrs. Sarah
27 Boucher, W., electrn.
29 Naylor, G. A.
45 Kinkead, Kenneth
47 Vacant
49 Chambers, D.
51 Hutchinson, Mrs. Mabel
53 Sinclair, Alex., grocer

...Here is Victoria Avenue..
55-85 Code BT4 1QW
55 Launderette
57 M'Ferran, Jas., brass mldr
59 Snodden, A.
61 Caruth, John, salesman
63 Pinkerton, Thomas, elect. welder
65 Ross, John
67 Lyons, Miss Madge
69 Curtis, Mrs. Rosamond
71 Burstow, Wm., hairdresser
73 Robinson, Miss Mar
75 Graham, W. J., textile wkr.
77 Graham, Mrs. Mabel
77a Patterson, Miss Emily
79 Cummings, Miss Sarah E
81 Crooks, George D., van driver
83 Fordham, Robert, salesman
85 Vacant ground

2-36 Code BT4 1QU
2 Occupied
4 Stewart, Mrs. Norma
6 M'Ferran, Robert, joiner
8 Occupied
10 Roberts, G.
12 Stitt, James
14 Russell, J.
16 Kitson, Mrs. Susannah
18 Simpson, James, joiner
20 M'Kendry, Mrs. Elizabeth
22 M'Carthy, J., wages clerk
24 Callaghan, John, engr
26 Yendall, George, manager
28 Nimick, Denis
30 Liddell, William, draughtmn
32 Shanks, Mrs. June

....Here is Vidor Gardens...
34 Wallace, William
36 Foreman, Samuel, joiner

38-104 Code BT4 1QW
38 Wright, Thomas A., plumber
40 Larmour, W. engr
42 McMillan, James, joiner
44 Scott, Thos. W., htg. engr.
46 Vacant
46a Vacant
48 Murphy, David, butcher
50 Vacant
50a Boyle, Mrs. Gladis
52 Blackmore, Alfred H., htg. eng
54 McKervey, Barry
56 Stephens, James McD., postman
58 Stevenson, John T.
60 Pue, Robert
62 Small, H., painter and decorator
64 Young, Victor, shtmtlwkr
66 Harris, Ernest, electrician
68 Morrison, Herbert
70 Elliott, Noel, joiner
72 Fisher, Jim
74 Millar, Samuel, electrician
76 Hunter, Leslie
78 Gordon, Robert, shipwright
80 Henry, Robt. D., P.O. driver
82 Shields, Mrs.
84 M'Connell, T., painter
86 Pavis, James A., fitter
88 Morrow, H. W.
90 Stronge J. W. H., meter insp
92 Carson, R. B., B.Sc., mech. engineer
94 Monteith, Samuel, drghtsmn
96 Occupied
98 Milligan, George, manager
100 Burton, Thomas
102 Harper, Walter
104 Dougan, A. D. fitter

VICTORIA ROAD
(No. 2)

Off Queen's Road
Island, E. Belfast (U.K.);
Island (N.I.)

Harland & Wolff, Ltd.

VICTORIA SQUARE

Continuation of William St. South to 103 Victoria Street
Central, W. Belfast (U.K.);
Central (N.I.)

1-55 Code BT1 4QD
1-7 Coulter, J. E., Ltd., car sales
9-21 FRACKELTON, JOHN, & SON, LTD., Glass, Paint and Wallpaper Merchants. T.N.: 28026-7. Code BT1 4QE
23-27 Hurst, Charles, Ltd. (rear entrance)
29 Christadelphian Hall
31-35 Chichester House (rear entrance)
37-41 M'Granaghan, D., turf accountant
43 Belfast City & District Water Commissioners (night office)
45-47 QUALITY CAFE & GRILL SNACKS, THE, T.N.: 30726
49 MOLEY'S MOTORS, Car Hirers. T.N.: 33123-4
51-55 Vacant ground

2-14 Littlewood Stores
.....Here is Telfair Street......
18-34 Code BT1 4QA
18 Conlan, James, Ltd., publcns.
CHURCHILL HOUSE
All P.O. Depts.—Code BT1 4BA
Ground Floor
Victoria Square Branch Post Office
"First Floor-Seventh Floor" Post Office Departments
All Ministry Offices—Code BT1 4QW
Eighth Floor
Ministry of Finance—Architects Branch
Ninth Floor
Ministry of Finance — Contracts Branch
Tenth Floor
Ministry of Finance — Works Administration
Eleventh Floor
Ministry of Finance — Architects Branch
Twelfth Floor
Ministry of Finance — Architects Branch
Thirteenth Floor
Ministry of Finance — Quantity Surveyor
Fourteenth Floor
Ministry of Finance—Electrical Engineering Department
Fifteenth Floor
Ministry of Finance—Electrical Engineering Department
Sixteenth Floor
Ministry of Finance—Electrical Engineering Department
Seventeenth Floor
Ministry of Finance — Plant Officer
36-40 Code BT1 4QB
36 Vacant
„ Kiosk, The, newsagents and confectioners
First Floor
„ COSELEY BUILDINGS (NORTHERN IRELAND) LTD., Structural Steel Contractors. T.N.: 32059
„ Vacant
Second Floor
Vacant
„ Lee, E., & Co., law searchers. Code BT1 4QY.
„ Ellis, law searchers. BT1 4QX

Belfast Street Directory listing Churchill House

smaller version of action man. We loved all this militairy stuff so try and imagine what it was like to us when the British Army arrived with all their gear and armoured cars. It was bloody heaven. Now Scelf had two brothers whom I was very friendly with and with Jim I still have contact with his sister Karen. Sadly Jim was killed in a tragic accident at school and although this happened thirty years ago I can assure you there is not a single day that goes by that I do not think of him. In the next floor down there was the Brady's one of whom was not only extremly close to my brother Liam but to our whole family. Now I know there was a sister but the only ones I remember were Alec, Jim and Henry whom we referred to as Hen. Hen never lived in his own flat but always stayed in ours. Hen and my brother Liam were friends and were never apart and this included staying together. These flats had two bed-rooms and in one was mum and dad and in the other was me, brother Liam and his mate Hen. For me it was bloody hell as both were older than me and I can state that I hated them both.

Now you probably think that I am being over the top here but allow me to explain. Many people remember the old tin baths and filling them up with boiling water from the open fire. Now I know I have pointed out that we had running hot water it did come from an immersion heater and therefore cost dosh. I can only

Hen, Me, Mum and Liam

Liam, Terry O'Neill (5d), Hen, Mum and Brendan O'Neill

Mum with Henry (Hen) Brady. Sadly Hen was to take his own life

No idea who the 'hard woman' is but that's me with mum in the background

Photograph showing the old Barrack Wall in the mid 1970's. Our tower block is to the left. To the extreme right (out of sight) was where McGurk's Bar stood and next to this again St Patrick's Primary School.

remember Saturday night in our flat and when we came in it was time to settle down. Now everything was worked out as Saturday night was TV night with Brucie's Generation Game and then a horror film of some sort. Before that it was bath time and this was the way it worked. First was dad before he went out and then mum. Then it was my brother Liam and my new found 'brother' Hen and then it was me. Now I know what your thinking and it's along the lines of new bath water and new hot water. Think again! It was the same bloody bath water and I was the bloody last one in. Not only was it dirty but was also freezing. Worse was to come in terms of clothing. Lets put it this way I was running about in Bay City Roller gear in 1977 so say no more about hand-me-downs!

Now I can move down the flats and tell about people I knew from the floors downwards but as I mentioned if I were to do this then I would be here for quite a while and although I knew people I only want to focus in on the people who I am extremely close to at the time of writing. In number 10 was the Uprichard's and although I was to become involved with their mum in community work in later years it's my age group I must stay with. Here there were two and that was Tom and Elaine and although not close friends I would never pass them. Facing them was the Hillis family with dad Jim being a caretaker of the flats for a while so he must've really hated us. They had a son in 1971 who went on to become a well known solicitor so I guess high rise living was not all that bad!

In the next landing (floor) we had the Wood's and all were well liked in the area. I can honestly say today that I have never met a nicer family in my life and I'm sure all those who grew up in Churchill will agree.

In the next floor down we had the Field's family. Leaving aside mum and dad we had John, Jim, Gary, Mark and Perry and although I was the same age as Gary it was Jim I was most friendly with. Facing the Fields was the Malone's. To be honest I don't know how to begin here but I have spoken to Matthew and he has laughed about it and give me the go ahead. The Malone's consisted of mum, dad as well as Martine, Matthew, Kevin and Martin. Now all are lovely people but Matthew was a different colour to the the rest and that was something we focused in on. Now don't get me wrong but at this time this seemed normal and we need to remember, as I have previously stated, kids are indeed the cruellest. I had one ear bigger than the other and I got hell over that so imagine what it must've been like if someone was a different colour!

Down below was number 7 and here lived the McFarlen's, Tohill's and the famous Rene Ringroad. Rene was a community activist and looking back now I can only admire what she did. She got the name 'Ringroad' because she was one of the people which stated that the Westlink was going to be built over their dead bodies. Well, you're not going to believe this, but the Westlink was built and it attracted at lot of attention because it went by our flats. Now this attention consisted of a lot of media and the people protesting whom

Our tower block today with the Westlink running straight past it - so I guess the protest failed!

I referred to as 'they' were our mum's and dad's so try and imagine how 'scundered' we were at the end of each protest day!

In number six the only person I remember was Tommy Duff and his family. The reason I know Tommy was because he went on to become the caretaker of Churchill after Mr Hillis. In landing number five was Jean Kelly and her family at 5b. She was Peter McBride's mum and Peter was later shot dead by trigger happy British soldiers a few years later. I don't know if it's true or not but I seem to remember her dad living to over 100. Across the way was the O'Neill family which consisted

The Unity Flats Complex

of Sean, Paul, Terry and Brendan. I was to become close friends with Paul (Bouncer) and Terry (Big Na) and we remain close friends to this day. The landing below at number four was mainly old people but at number 4a lived Mrs Gowdey. My memories here are of her falling out of her window and being killed as she washed them. Number three and two was also elderly people as was almost all of number one with the exception of a friend who lived at number 1b. Hugh (Piper) Morrison and I were to be friends for many years and I remember he had a sister who lived in the Unity Flats complex. When me and Piper knocked about together over there our friends included Harry Hale and 'Big' Jake O'Rawe.

This brings us to the ground floor of Churchill House. Unlike the upper floors which had four flats this only had two. We were at G1 which was designed as the caretakers flat and which had two bedrooms the same as all those above. Next door at G2 was only a one bedroom flat and quite a few people lived here over the years and I think, because of the one bedroom, it must have been designed for a single person. The main family I remember who lived here were the McCullough's. The reason they stick in my mind was because I hung around with their son Eddie (Big Ed) and because there were so many of them in here. If memory serves me right there was mum and dad, three sisters and two brothers living in this one bedroomed gaff so I'm sure that was a bundle of laughs for all concerned!

AROUND THE BLOCK

We thought of Churchill House as our own private domain but of course we all had our friends beyond it. To the front of our block facing the Antrim Road was the Carlisle Estate. As I mentioned when we first moved into the flats there was a section of the old Victoria Barracks remaining. When this was demolished the Carlisle Estate was built and opened in 1969. Needless to say the kids in this estate were the same kids we were to go to school with and depending which primary school you went to was the main factor on who you knocked about with. My friends from the new estate were to be Michael Campbell, Martin 'Dixie' Dornan, Bill 'Minty' Murray, 'Big' Rab Craig, Paddy Brown and Harry Wylie. Harry and I were basically up to everything but in later years it was his older brother John 'Junior' whom I was to become extremely good friends with – with the exception of the time he grassed us all up to the peelers but that's another story!

To the right of our block was Victoria Parade and all the other tower blocks which made up the estate. Also at this side beyond the tower blocks was the New Lodge Road and the long Victorian streets which ran parallel with it. It's worth pointing out that there are many who state that they are from the Barrack and not the New Lodge. The Barrack, as the name would suggest, was built on the site of the massive Victoria Barracks most of which was destroyed during the German Blitz on Belfast in 1941. I would tend to agree but while I say that I'm from the Barrack I state that it is part of the greater New Lodge area. I know many will totally disagree with me but that's just my opinion.

In the parade my closest friend for many years was Kevin 'Hazzel' Morgan with our other friends living in the tower blocks being Phil 'Doc" Doherty who lived in Templar and John 'Bugsy' McAuley who lived in Artillery. Most of us had very few friends in the long streets but I had a few with Joe 'Joesh' Thompson, Patrick 'Doc' Martin, Patrick 'Buckwheat' Martin and Eddie Kane being the few that spring to mind. Eddie and I were friends long before this when he lived directly behind our tower block. Eddie's father was one of those killed in the McGurk's Bar bomb and his brother Billy was later shot dead by loyalists as he lay sleeping.

Also on Victoria Parade was a complex which was to play a massive part in all our lives – The Recy. This was opened in 1960 as the City of Belfast Recreation Centre and was designed as a physical training depot

Photograph taken from Churchill House around 1967 showing the remaining section of Victoria Barracks. When this was demolished the present Carlisle Estate was built

Gymnasium equipment being moved into The Recy on its opening.
Below - The main hall of The Recy

The old Barrack Wall at North Queen Street

The old football pitch which was at the back of Churchill House

Looking towards Victoria Parade

The 'slide' which was at the back of Duncairn Parade. A sloped concrete area this kept up occupied for hours when we slid down in with bits of cardboard and old milk crates

mainly for kids. When our tower block was built next to it it became our second home. When we played in it there was all the stuff you would expect to find in a well fitted out gymnasium ranging from climbing frames right though to massive swinging ropes. What I do remember is that every single day someone got hurt but those days you simply cried for a while and got on with it or if it was more serious up to the Mater. Today's 'anything for a claim' brigade would have loved it. The Recy is one of the oldest buildings in the whole area as it is one of the few remaining buildings of the old Victoria Barracks when it was the army gymnasium. It closed down in the mid 1970's for a major renovation and reopened a few years later as North Queen Street Community Centre but it is still known by its proper name of The Recy. When it reopened all the gym gear and deadly swings were all gone and it was simply never the same however it was here in a few years that my very long career as a community worker was to begin.

Another view of 'The Pitch' looking towards St Patrick's

Looking towards Glenravel Street from Churchill House

Behind our flats was the North Queen Street and Sailortown areas. Sailortown was never known to us as that and the whole area was just known as The Docks. Also at this part of the block was our school, St Patrick's, and the areas around that.

To the left hand side was what we called the 'Oldies' which was Clifton House, an old people's home. This was the old Belfast Poor House and beside it was all its farming grounds including livestock. When we played here the old pig sties (without the pigs of course) remained and these kept us occupied for hours with one of our many 'wars' with a few unfortunates stuck in the sty as the enemy while we bricked and bricked it until our arms were sore. All this area was extremely over-grown and the whole place totally fascinated us. The caretaker at the time lived in the old gate lodge and if memory serves me right his name was Paddy Murphy – that man must have really hated us.

'The Swings' which were put onto the waste field next to our flats - one fall from these and you really knew all about it!

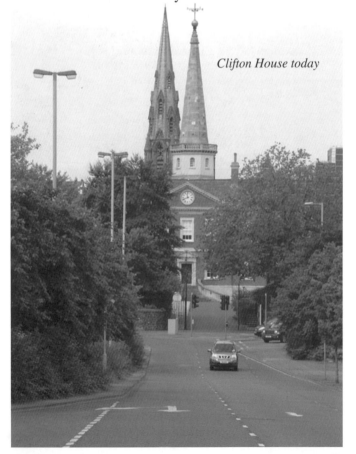

Clifton House today

Between Clifton House and our block on North Queen Street were a fantastic row of Georgian houses which had a couple of sweet shops in them. The shops in question were extremely easy to nick from (so I hear) and that is why we spent so much time around them. Across the street was our school and the Loughran's shop which I have previously mentioned. Next to this was the old Tin Hut which was exactly that – built of tin (well corrugated iron but you get the picture). This was some sort of community hall but do you know I can never remember being in it once. On the other side was a shop which I think was Collins' and then another row of houses until we got to Frederick Street with Brennan's Bar at the corner which, surprise surprise, was destroyed in a bomb attack. Crossing over was St Kevin's Hall which belonged to the nearby St Patrick's Chapel and next to this was the corner shop of Mays & Kays. Like the shops across the way this was very easy to nick out off and on one occasion I remember one of our gang being sent in to nick a packet of Snowballs. He came out with a packet of Paris Buns and was sent back, with the Paris Buns, to put them back and get Snowballs which he did. This brought us on to Donegall Street and where the Rio Café was situated with Marty Quinn's barber shop next door. This is where every kid in the district got their hair cut and Marty's is still going to this day further down the street. A few doors down was St Patrick's Chapel and my main memories of this was how to avoid it and I was not alone. Every Sunday

The Recy

Enjoying the ropes inside the Recy

our parents would send us down with collection envelopes to go to chapel and to drop the said envelope into the collection plate. Now do I really need to spell out what in fact really happened!

Up behind Clifton House was Glenravel Street and Henry Place. It was here that we had institutions such as the Benn Hospital, Belfast High School, Our Lady of Mercy School, Clifton Hotel and Glenravel Street R.U.C. Barracks which I will touch on later. Behind this was Clifton Street Cemetery which I will also

mention later but our very early memories from it are when the British Army moved into the Glenravel Barracks (well actually a special needs school next door). In the cemetery they had rows of trip wire which, when touched, sent a flare screaming into the sky. Have a quick guess what one of our favourite past times was? On the cemetery wall was an army observation post and when we were in the cemetery we would hear this loud English accent shouting "Playing in the churchyard – ger outta of it." Which we didn't!

Aerial photograph of our area in 1960. Construction work on the first tower block can be seen at the bottom right and the spot where our tower block was to be built is marked with the X. To the left is Clifton House and behind that Glenravel Street and Clifton Street Cemetery. The remaining section of Victoria Barracks can clearly be seen as can what was known as 'Archie's Dam' above it.

DEATH-TRAPS AND CASUALTY

Is it me or is childhood fast becoming a thing of the past? These days I get the impression that kids don't want to be kids for long and only seem to do so when they are playing their computer games behind closed doors. In our childhood there was only one play ground and that was the one in North Queen Street. I use the term playground lightly because some of the items in it were real death traps. There was a slide which must have been at least thirty feet high and if you fell off it you were doomed. Then there was the dreaded witches hat, the purpose of which I could never understand, but it seem that you had to knock each other off and broken fingers or toes were always guaranteed. When we were kids we were up to something every single day ranging from games of kick the tin, two man hunt and building guiders. Now guiders were basically made up of old pram wheels, a plank, bolt and lots of nails. Although numerous attempts were made none ever had brakes. At the back of the flats was a brilliant hill for guider purposes, which took you from Carlisle Road right down to North Queen Street through a spiral of hills. These had to be mastered because if they were not then you were straight off the Barrack Wall (which had a drop of about ten feet) and therefore a quick visit to the Mater Hospital afterwards. The good thing about that time was that cars were not seen as a threat as there were very few people in the whole estate who actually had one. On top of this the area was usually sealed off with numerous barricades or nearby bomb scares. But back to my point of guiders and the biggest threat to their runs was not cars but these bleeding barricades which were erected all over the place. You see, to get a good guider run you needed a steep hill which ended in something straight or even a waste field (remember lack of brakes!)

Back in our area we had a series of slopes known as the seven hills. Looking back today I can conclude that whoever named them this obviously had difficulty in the maths department, as there are only five of them. These began just outside the religious grotto near Duncairn Parade and ended at Artillery Flats. Once at the last hurdle you had a choice. You could go straight on and your guider would have come to a safe stop outside Artillery Youth Club or you could have went left and guaranteed yourself an instant injury. Turning left brought you on to the steepest of the hills and your braking system was none other than the wall around Artillery Flats. Of course every guider driver choose the left turn as going the safe way was never an option. Looking back I often wonder at the amount of injuries which were caused because of this but I also remember members of a nearby rival gang in the seven hills area having two mattresses at the bottom of the said hill – bleeden wimps!

The play park on North Queen Street. Sadly the thirty foot high slide and witches hat are out of view

Sadly guiders are no more as kids today don't seem to have the imagination to play Hingo or Two Man Hunt let along build a guider. Even bikes seem to have lost their entertainment edge as many kids throw their cycles into the garden shed once it gets so much as a puncture. What seem to be in nowadays are the motorised death traps they seem to speed about on and all the electronic games which keeps them in front of televisions and computers for hours. Ask any kid what Kick the Tin is and his reply will be along the lines of some X Box game!

One thing that was always guaranteed during our playtimes was a visit to casualty. There were odd occasions when we had to be kept in hospital and I can tell you now that there was one period up in the wards when I would rather have been back at school. Those who remember me from my education days will know how extreme that comment is!

Around the mid 1970's I sort of burned the lower part of my right leg pretty badly while messing about with some matches and a number of combustible materials. Without going into great detail (more on this later) what began was the first of a series of operations that were hell at the time and which still effect me to this day (for some reason the cold weather makes me limp!) I woke up and my leg was three times its size with a load of bandages around it but unknown to me worse was to come. The first operation was to do something to prepare my leg for something or other but it was the result of the second operation that was to mentally scar me for life. This operation was a skin graft which was taking skin from my thigh to put over the damaged area of my lower leg so now I had two areas of bleedin pain to contend with. Anyway I was still in hospital and looking back I have no idea for how long but to give you an idea I missed a year in school so that will give an indication of my stay. I can remember the nurses and such like were not allowed anywhere near my actual burn as the dressings could only be changed by specialists but they could change the dressing on my skin graft which, as I stated, was on my thigh.

One day I was taken for a bath by the Matron who was a nun and she had me get in and steep in it for a while. The lower part was never to go into the water so she had to put me in with the lower part of my right leg out of the water so she had to hold it out. Now my only interest was to cover my willie and that is what I done as I am a shy person but what was ahead of me knocked that thought straight out of my head. The Matron was to change the dressing on my skin graft and it was this dressing which was allowed to steep and she had to remove the old dressing while keeping the lower part of the same leg out of the water. This she did but her removal technique was unique to say the least as she gripped the upper end of it and ripped it off in one go.

There is no doubt that my screams where heard throughout the hospital and take my word for it that was one hell of an experience and the pain was really something else. Now I may appear as if I'm getting a dig at the hospital but believe me when I point out that I'm not. In those days we took that treatment for granted and we were happy for getting it but looking back we must have caused the hospital more problems than we did our parents. Another of our past times was a stone war and people today may find this pretty hard to grasp but it's exactly what it sounds like! We would arrange two teams on the old waste grounds on what is now the Westlink and place an item such as an old pram or milk crate at a section of it. The teams then had to part and when it reached a certain time or if something was shouted then it was time to obtain the said item. The rules were simple yet brutal. Each team had to get the item back to their 'camp' to win and the rules for doing so were non existent - in other words by whatever means necessary! This always resulted in a stone war where we literally threw bricks at each other and if you think that was bad you should have seen the close up combat! Needless to say injuries occurred and where was it the causalities went? - Yes the Mater Hospital! So can you blame the old matrons? Looking back they must have been sick of the sight of us.

Another occasional past time was 'Catties.' These were home made catapults which were deadly. It was the usual story of a small home-made steel frame from an old spring bed, elastic bands and the actual 'bullets' were cut up strips of copper wire. To this day I can never understand how none of us ever lost an eye because it was never for the want of trying! If you thought that was bad then you have never seen the infamous 'rubber band gun.' This was was a simple length of wood with two nails in it hammered in at an angle. The rubber bands were obtained from the light fittings in the tower blocks and from the pipes which were used in the construction of the Westlink. The bands would be stretched between the nails and to fire it all you had to do was aim the stick, flick the band over the nail and bingo - absolute agony for your unfortunate victim. Believe it or not we actually devised an automatic version where several bands were stretched over larger nails and up to three bands could be fired at one time at one victim. To describe us as mad would be an understatement - we were absolutely bonkers and how we lived this long is an out and out miracle!

That's what we did for fun in our childhood and that's just the liberal stuff as I dare make no mention of the kidnappings, beatings and general all round suffering we inflicted on each other - and that was among friends so is it really any wonder that old matron treated us how she did!

Map of the New Lodge area in 1960. The Barrack area is under construction on the site of the old Victoria Barracks

A PUNCH, A SLAP AND A GOOD OLD FASHIONED BOOT IN THE ARSE!

Over the past few years there has been quite a lot of debate over the parents right to hit their children as punishment and there seems to be a great division on the issue. To be honest I don't see the harm in a good smack across the back of the legs but when a parent turns to their children in anger then that is wrong. To say my dad gave me a slap on the back of the wrist would be one hell of an understatement as these were the days when if you were suspected of wrong doing then you were slaughtered. I did not make a mistake when I said 'suspected' because then suspicion was enough and if you were later found innocent then you were informed that the punishment was something else that you may have got away with. The bottom line was if you were a kid growing up at this time then the word fairness may as well have been in Russian.

I was no angel and not only was I a terror to my mum and dad but to the whole district but I would like to take this opportunity to point out two things. Compared to what kids are doing today I may as well have been in the Salvation Army and 80% of the stuff I got the blame on had absolutely nothing to do with me but in those days such a technicality didn't matter. When you got a 'hiding' of your da for something that you did then fairs fair but it was a real downer when it was for nothing. My da was a strange person when it came to all this because some of the things he hit me for were quite unique to say the least. Allow me to explain. One day I was on the waste field near my house playing with my Action Man (looted from the Co-op of course!) when one of the local kids came over to me. Both of us started playing together for quite a while when suddenly things turned sour. I was hit on the leg with a stone and my Action Man went flying over the wall of the nearby Peeler Barrack. Needless to say I went home crying and told dad what had happened. I was instantly grabbed by the scruff, thrown out the door and told to go and sort this person out and if need be to use a brick. So out I went, grabbed a halfer (half a brick for today's generation) and hit my foe on the back of the head with it. Five minutes later the dad from the other side was down at our door with his child and informed my dad what had happened. The beating I got was unbelievable. And for what? After all I did exactly what I was told!

Another day at school me and a few friends were watching the snow falling outside and decided the next day to go on the 'beak' so that we could have some fun with the said snow. Next day we did exactly that and went to the local graveyard and threw snowballs at people passing on the Antrim Road. A few hours later two of us decided to go up to the Waterworks and mess about. On the upper pond we were doing this on the ice when suddenly it gave way and yours truly fell through. To this day I remember the coldness and I can tell you it was bleeden cold. In those days Snorkels were the height of fashion (hooded rain coats with fur around the rim). I had one on and had I not then you wouldn't be reading this today as it kept me afloat and stopped me drowning. My mate, Sean Collins, who was with me was laughing hysterically but when he saw me lose consciousness he then hurried for help. I was rushed to hospital and all I remember was waking up three days later in intensive care at the Mater with loads of heaters around me and being suffocated by the piles of blankets on top of me. I soon learned that I was clinically dead for five minutes and that if I had not reached hospital when I did then I would have been in the ice rink in the sky. Mum and dad were outside and when I came round they were sent for. Mum hugged and kissed me like mad as could be expected but dad's reaction was quite different. He told me then when I got home I was dead for going on the 'hike' from school and take my word for it he stuck by his word.

Another accident which had me getting a good hiding was extremely tragic for the person involved but had absolutely nothing to do with me. The 'Painty' was a waste ground on North Queen Street where a paint store had stood before being blown up by the IRA. I actually remember this bombing not only because it burned for days but because in the following days nearly everyone was out painting their front doors and window frames. Needless to say the site was cleared and lay derelict until houses were built on it in the mid 80's. One day a lad from our school called Joe went there and was trapped under fallen masonry. Locals rushed to his rescue but sadly he was killed. Needless to say word went round very quickly and when it reached our house they were told it was me. Mum went into severe shock and was taken to hospital and dad was one of those who rushed to the scene. We had been playing kick about at the back of Alexander Flats when we heard about the accident and immediately went down to see what was going on. When I got there my dad grabbed me and screamed "you wee b*****d, have you any idea what you've done to your mother?" and proceeded to kick me all the way home. So here I was getting a beating for not being killed. It could only happen to me!

While on the subject many school kids may find it hard to believe but in these days you got hit in school with the infamous strap. One of my old teachers reminded me recently of my reply to a slapping. What they usually heard was I'm getting my da on you or my big brother who's in the 'Ra but I was reminded of one of my replies. After getting 'six of the best' I threatened the teacher "when I grow up I'm gonna knock your ******** in." Now beat that for a threat!

EARNING AN HONEST PENNY
(WELL ALMOST!)

I am well aware that this is not going to refer to everyone reading this but one thing I want people from working class communities around my age to admit is how many were involved in the nicking of copper and lead from old derelict buildings? If you have answered honestly then I'm sure the figure is pretty high. The reason I know this is I was one such person and during the 1970's it seemed to me as though everyone was at it.

Being from the Barrack area at that time a lot of buildings were being vacated for the construction of the Westlink Motorway and a lot of derelict buildings meant a lot of lead and copper. It was a thriving business and what it involved was securing a building and stripping as much lead and copper in the shortest possible time before word got around that there was a way in. Looking back there is no doubt that this was extremely dangerous as you were not quite sure if the electric was switched off when ripping out copper wire and as for climbing on to roofs to strip off the lead - well that speaks for itself.

The way the lead market worked was quite simple. You got the lead, bunged it into an old pram or trolly of some sort and took it to the nearest scrapyard. Here it was weighed and you were given money for it. Copper was slightly different. It was worth more and if you got copper water pipes you were OK but if it was copper wire then you had to burn off the rubber coating on a fire in waste ground which caused a lot of black smoke and therefore the attention of the Peelers. We had two nearby scrapyards and both were in Great George's Street. One was at the corner of Thomas Street and the other, known as Cookes, was further down. We were always asked where we got the stuff from and they always received the bog standard answer - found it!

We lived in Churchill Flats which is now directly next to the Westlink and in those days we had the perfect view of the buildings being vacated. When the removal lorries moved in we were quite often watching them and when they moved off we were straight down and in behind them. One such case was an old warehouse in Great George's Street. Inside there was a massive slide from the top of the building to the bottom which was used for sliding down sacks of grain and as we were still kids a lot of fun was had on that. One day, when the Peelers came, it proved useful for a quick getaway but unfortunately for us it also led to a quick capture as it brought us straight into the arms of the cops waiting at the bottom of it. We were never scooped but instead you got a quick size ten in the arse

department and a good old fashioned slap across the head. The parting comments from the Peelers were along the lines of if we came back we would be arrested but as soon as they went we were straight in behind them - although not using the slide for future getaways!

Back to the business side of things and the copper and lead. These old warehouses were coming down with the stuff. The most prized items were the lead sheeting off the flat roofs. If you got this then it meant that you could wrap it around 'bessy bars and bring it to the scrapyard for weighing. OK, this might be wiping their eye but do you really think they were giving us kids the full price of the material? Now I know many people are wondering what a 'bessy bar' is. Well they were the iron weights used in the old sash windows and which were quite heavy. In addition to copper piping there was also the old lead piping to be got. This was a real dirty job as it often meant digging it out of walls and getting soaked into the bargain.

One thing I do remember from all this was someone seemed to have ended up in hospital almost everyday. The most common injury was the nail in the foot and almost all of us have the scars on the soles of our feet to prove it. I remember one member of our lead gang getting a massive nail straight through his foot. It must have been extremely painful because his lead collecting days and messing about in old buildings ceased from that day on. My own brother Liam was another major causality. He was up stripping a roof when he slid, fell off and went straight through another roof a few floors down. Covered in blood he managed to stagger up to our flat from where our Da took him up to the Mater Hospital. It's a miracle he did not bleed to death because my Da (being my Da) decided to stop and talk to everyone he met on the way up. Needless to say my Da told Liam in no uncertain terms that if he ever caught him at any 'oul' buildings he would get much worse.

This brings me to another old building which came onto the lead market - Glenravel Street Barracks. The Peelers moved out of this in 1971 and moved into the recently constructed North Queen Street. The lead on this barrack roof was tremendous and because it was overlooked by our flats then we were the first on the scene. We went straight for the roof and the lead gang consisted of me, my brother Liam and Henry 'Hen' Brady. Looking back I have no idea why I ever went along with them because all I seemed to end up with was a bottle of Coke and bag of crisps. Anyway, we

Glenravel Street Peeler Barrack

went straight for the roof and were working away getting the lead off when shouts of "Liam, Liam" were heard coming from the street below. One extremely careful look over at the side of a downpipe revealed it to be our Da. At this exact moment we did not know it but one of the rival lead gangs went and told our Dad that were were there so that they could muscle in behind us - it was a cut throat market.

This was a major problem and if you think Hen was okay then you would be wrong. Hen had two brothers and one sister and lived with his mum and dad in a two bedroom flat in number 11 Churchill Flats. Because he was never out of our house (and this included sleeping there) then my Dad would have had no hesitation in giving him the same treatment as me and Liam. We were in trouble and it seemed to be getting worse with the shouts became threats to come up. Suddenly Liam turned to me and said for me to go down and pretend that I was on my own. "No bloody way"

was my instant reply which I thought was reasonable, sensible and less painful for me. "You're the smallest and there is no way Da will give you a kicking" was Liam's reasoning. After a short time I was left with no choice and on the promise of some money for the lead instead of the sweets I went down. I came out of the building and I can honestly state that I was convinced I was not going to get touched. I was grabbed by the hair with my Da screaming into my face "where's Liam?" "He's not in there" was my reply "I'm just playing on my own." For someone convinced by his older and more sensible brother that I would not be touched I can clearly state that a painful lesson was learned that day. I can truthfully say that my feet did not touch the ground between the Peeler barrack and our flat.

Later on Liam and Hen came in stuffing their faces with all sorts of sweets and lemonade. "Where's mine" I asked. "Sorry kid, you weren't there," was the simple reply. Well I did say it was a cut throat market!

THE TROUBLES

In the Summer of 1969 a new conflict broke out in Northern Ireland which became known as The Troubles and at the time it was thought that it would last no more than a few months but in fact it lasted for almost forty years. Much has been written about this conflict without me giving you a history lesson on it but there is no doubt that this was to play a massive part in my life. Another thing that I could do is write about my experiences of growing up in The Troubles but even that would take up a lot more pages than what's in this entire book!

What I have decided to do is try to describe what it was like and also to write about a few of the events which stick in my head. This is not intended to be a history of The Troubles in the New Lodge area as once again this would make up quite a compressive read!

I was four when the Northern Ireland conflict erupted and the area in which I lived was to become one which was to suffer tremendously. For example more people were killed within the New Lodge area than anywhere else of a similar size in the whole of the North. It was the area which saw the first use of rubber bullets, the first use of nightsight sniper rifles by the British army and was the area in which the first British soldier was killed in the conflict. Needless to say the rest of North Belfast told a similar story and throughout The Troubles it was the most dangerous place to live.

The Humber which was known as a 'Pig'

A Saracen which we called a 'sixer' because of its six wheels

A Ferret

A Saladin

One minute we were playing with toy soldiers and action men the next the real thing was on our streets

A Scooby-Doo armoured bulldozer

A Scooby-Doo removes a burnt out bus from North Queen Street. A 'sixer' can be seen in the background outside the old Gem Bar

Growing up as children the whole lot to us was very exciting. Here was us playing with toy soldiers and action men and then seeing the real thing on our doorstep. Try and imagine what it was like watching military helicopters landing on the roof of our flats to build look out posts. Needless to say soldiers where everywhere and in all sorts of armoured cars which we had our own names for such as pigs, sixers and whippets. Belfast in the 1970's was not the place to be but for us we had no choice as we lived here. As previously mentioned one of my early memories of The Troubles was the bombing of McGurk's Bar which was the first of the major atrocities and which saw 15 local people dead and countless injured but sadly many more were to come.

As children we had to work out who was who and who was fighting who. We knew the basics which were that the IRA were fighting the British army but there were two of them – Official (who were known as the Sticks) and Provisional IRA (who were known as the Provos). Then they would fight each other and then another split saw the INLA who became known as the Erps. Then there was the UVF who were shooting Catholics as well as the UDA who were doing the same as well as marching everywhere. We had not got a clue!

Needless to say there were events which we had heard about but didn't really understand until we got older. I'm talking about events such as Bloody Sunday and

Internment. One series of events which I remember well but didn't really understand was what went on to become known as Bloody Friday.

On that day bombs seemed to have been going off everywhere in what was a major attack on Belfast by the IRA. Nine people were killed and although looking back it seemed to have went on forever it only lasted 75 minutes.

Closer to home there was also a major incident in our own area when six people were shot dead by both the British army and loyalists. They became known as the New Lodge Six. As a child I remember my older brother bringing us up to the old National School on the New Lodge Road and showing us the bullet holes on the wall and if my memory serves me right there were dozens of them. There was also the up close and personal stuff. I remember a friend and I hanging around outside Artillery Flats and this guy going over towards another. Next thing a gun was pulled out and one of them was shot dead. It all happened so quickly but I can picture every second in my head today as I was less than ten feet away. The guy who was shot dead was Seamus McCusker, a Sinn Fein leader in the area. He had been killed by the Official IRA. I don't know if it was because they controlled our area of the New Lodge but the Official IRA always seemed to have been the most feared. I had many a run in with them as a child and none more memorable than the time I nicked two of their guns. A friend and I were playing about in the washhouses of Artillery Flats when we came across two handguns. Thinking they were toys we took one each, openly played with them, and then went about our merry way. As you would imagine the Sticks were not a happy bunch. They had heard about us playing with them and set out to find us. Because my friend lived in Artillery Flats he was easily got and they got that handgun back and then they came for me.

A British soldier on patrol on the New Lodge Road, 1970

Briting soldiers arrest a man on the New Lodge Road

Rioting on North Queen Street with Artillery Flats to the left

British soldier on patrol on Victoria Parade. Churchill House can be seen in the background (far left)

The Starry Plough bar on the New Lodge Road complete with wall to prevent bomb attack. Needless to say it was bombed and I remember my mum running over to it thinking dad was in it. Thankfully he had just left

The Dempsey family

An injured British soldier being taken away from Artillery Flats

Patroling the remains of the old Fenian Gut area

British soldiers at the junction of New Lodge Road and Lepper Street

Junction of Annadale Street and Antrim Road

British Paratroopers in Carlisle Estate

Junction of New Lodge Road and Antrim Road

For us kids it wasn't all bad!

They grabbed me in the Recy and took me to an upstairs room. There they slapped me about until I told them that I had put it back and that I would take them to it. They then took me to Artillery Flats and when I got to the landing I made a bolt for it. I ran down the stairs and straight home where I told my dad what was going on. He hit the roof when I told them that they had beat me and he asked me where the gun was. I went and got it and gave it to my dad who in turn had handed it over to the Provos. When the Sticks came banging on our door my dad went through them for hitting me and told them that the Provos had it and to take it up with them. Needless to say there was nothing they could do about it as the Provos were a bigger organisation with more guns! Dad later told me that if they had come and asked for it without hitting me then he would have handed it over. Bear in mind that at the time I was seven or eight years of age and getting hit by grown men. Over the years while playing we found everything from guns right through to mortars but I can assure you that they were left where they were and we got as far away from them as we could.

As previously mentioned there were numerous incidents around our area which saw people being killed and places being blown to bits. Another of these incidents which stuck in my mind was the murders of the Dempsey family in Hillman Street. This happened in August 1976 when Loyalist's firebombed a house killing Joseph Dempsey, his wife and ten month old daughter. A totally innocent family killed as they lay sleeping.

One of the most sinister incidents occurred as we were making our way to school one morning. It was shortly after the IRA had bombed a hotel in East Belfast called La Mon killing twelve people. The RUC were stopping cars on North Queen Street and handing out leaflets for information on the bombing. These leaflets were in full colour and showed a badly burned body of one of the victims. Suddenly one of the RUC men began handing them to us kids and needless to say we took them with us to school. When our teacher saw them he was furious and after he collected them all together he brought them to the head master who in turn returned them to the nearby RUC barrack on North Queen Street where he made a complaint.

Today when I look back at all this I often wonder what it must have been like for our parents trying to bring us up and keep us safe while everything around us was being blown to bits. Because we lived quite close to the city centre we were hearing bombs go off almost every day. What the IRA were doing was striking at the economy by destroying businesses and shops. The shops where our favourite as on quite a few occasions we were in as soon as the firemen left. The main one

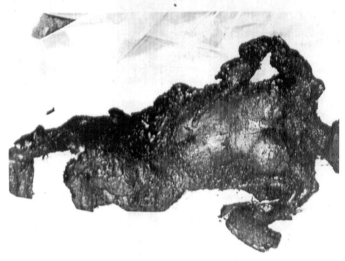

MURDER MURDER
MURDER MURDER MURDER MURDER
This is what the bombers did

to a human being
MURDER MURDER MURDER MURDER

which springs to mind was the bombing of the Co-op department store in nearby York Street. This was a massive shop which sold almost everything. After it was bombed we were in and naturally made our way to the toy department. Now bear in mind that this building had just been destroyed by bombs so the

The bombing of the Co-op

dangers were beyond belief. When we discovered the remains of the toy department I wanted to go for the Hornby Railways but this entire section was completely burned out. I was totally gutted but this was soon made up when we came across hundreds of Action Men and we took the lot. There were that many that we were taking them out of their boxes so as to make more room in our sacks so that we could take even more. When we were done we did not have individual Action Men to play with – we had armies of them!

Our Action Man collection was enhanced even more when the toy shop of Frederick Thomas was bombed in Royal Avenue when once again we went in and took all we could find. Now you could be forgiven for thinking that our parents must be uncaring if they let us do this but you take my word for it if any of us were found out we were doomed. The reason I say any of us

is because of the fact that we all lived in the one tower block. If one of us had been discovered then the other parents knew that we would all have been together and a swift beating would soon follow as well as the customary grounding for a week. You would also think that the emergence of hundreds of Action Men would also have been a bit of a give-away but if we were not caught red handed then we always had an excuse. The Action Men from the Co-op bombing were given to us by the soldiers guarding the remains and that was a story we stuck by because that really did happen. The troops would have taken stuff off looters caught coming out and while they copped the best gear they generally also gave the kids toys. Word got out that they were doing this and so when our parents heard it then our story was believed. The only snag was they were giving out one or two items of toys here and there not hundreds of bloody Action Men!

Now you must admit Belfast people really do have the best sense of humour as this sign placed on the remains of the Co-op shows!

WALKING WITH MOTHER!

Today we have a half decent travel system and part of that is the black taxi service. Now when I was a child this was certainly not the service it is today and operated only in West Belfast. For Northies that meant a trek to Castle Street where the taxis were lined up on one side of the road from Queen Street upwards. Coming from our house that meant a walk along North Queen Street, Carrick Hill (then called Upper Library Street) and Millfield. It's strange what sticks in your head and now that I'm looking back I can honestly state that I must have been traumatised by the stories my mother told me - as she walked me along it!

The first thing that comes to mind was the stories she told to me about the Shankill Butchers. Now remember I was only a kid and the Shankill Butchers to me was somewhere Protestants got their meat on the Saturday! I remember her telling me about one young man coming along with his girlfriend, both of them being attacked and he being killed in a horrific manner. What the hell was my mum telling me this for! Another of her stories were of the same murder gang going into a building and killing people, two of whom lived in the same estate as us. Was it any wonder I was terrified

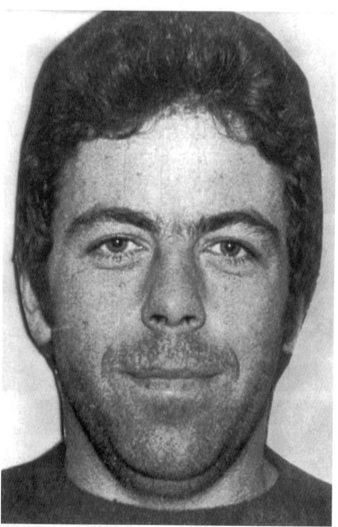

As a child Galloper Thompson was nothing - Lenny Murphy was the real Bogeyman!

My dad always believed that some soldiers should have been playing with Action Men instead of being them when he saw images such as this!

going along this bleeden street! On that occasion I now know what that she was referring to Lenny Murphy's sick squad who went into a bottling plant on Millfield and brutally murdered Frances Donnelly, Marie McGratten, Gerard Grogan and Thomas Osbourne. The last two were only teenagers and were the two she was referring to when she stated that they were from our estate. Now most people reading this would think that mum must have been pretty weird telling me this stuff but please allow me to explain what type of person she was.

My mum, along with my dad, were devout Catholics – something I did not take after them! At the height of what we call the Troubles they were outraged and horrified when anyone was killed just for their religion as they believed things like this belonged in the far past. At the height of these Troubles they believed that if anyone was killed because they were in the Provisional IRA, the Official IRA, UVF, INLA or UVF then that was fair as those people had made a decision to become involved in this conflict. But if someone was killed simply because of their religion then they believed that that was wrong and tried to tell us this through these horror stories. And that went both ways. If someone was killed simply because they were Protestants they were outraged. There are those in the Loyalist community who, because of some of the nonsense they are told, believe that everyone in the Catholic community celebrate Protestant deaths. Take my word for it when it came to the Shankill bomb, the Enniskillen bombing and many others the last place you wanted to be was in our house. My dad even went one step further as he was outraged every time a British soldier was killed. He fully understood the political meaning behind it all but when he heard of the ages of some of the troops killed his heart really went out to them and their families. He looked beyond the uniform and concentrated on the person inside it. I can still hear his voice in my head when I watch the news about Iraq and his comment of "for Gods sake they're only children, they should be playing with Action Men instead of being one!" He always told us that 99.9% of these soldiers didn't even want to be here and didn't give a damn about this place called Northern Ireland. His argument was that if we lived in a city across the water we could have been in the army and ended up in a place like this in the middle of a conflict we knew absolutely nothing about. I can tell you now - he was right. My son was in the Irish Army but what if we had moved to Liverpool as planned when me and my brother were children? I compile a chronology called The Troubles and when I look at the ages of people killed in conflict I just look and think that they are either the same age, or younger, of my youngest child!

Now on the way across towards the west it was daylight but when we were coming back it was always dark and we had to walk across in darkness due to, as I remember, lack of street lights. On one of these I can remember both of us being chased by a man who was calling us Provie ******** because I had a parka coat on. What was all that about! At that age I didn't even know who the Provies were and the only reason I had the said coat on was to keep warm. Apparently, I later learned, Republicans wore parka coats but surely this person must have seen that I was only a child and in those days you wore what was handed to you!

On our return journey we always walked on the city centre side as the other side was into the Brown Street area which of course was Protestant and which then connected to the Shankill. Now try and imagine how confusing this was for me. As a young child I had a friend in what later became the Shankill Estate and we would meet up every day by me calling to his house and playing in flats which were then under construction in the lower Shankill. We had great fun and all the political turmoil was well above our heads. To meet I would go across to Stanhope Street in the Unity Flats complex and up to the Shankill area and when he came to me it would be the same route only in the opposite direction. One day I remember going over to meet him and there was this massive barbed wire fence running from Clifton Street right across to Peter's Hill. I sat and looked at this thing for what must have seemed forever when my friend appeared at the other side wondering where I was.

Now here's the stuff writers love. Here was a young Catholic boy standing feet away from his Protestant friend with this massive barbed wire fence erected the night before in between them. I can tell you now that that absolutely gutted me and I know he felt the same because the tears sort of gave it away. The last I saw of him was as he walked back up towards the newly built flats and being approached by a few older boys. They saw him talking to me and beat him up.

Here was my closest friend who I spent every day with and the last I ever saw of him was getting punched and kicked and because of this stupid fence erected by the British Army and there was absolutely nothing I could do about it. What ever became of him I'll never know but believe it or not I still think of him to this very day. You may also think that with the resources available to me I would be able to trace him but the sickening thing is I don't even remember his name!

Now people are going to read this and state why did I just not meet him at Carlisle Circus? Well the answer is quite simple. I was five years old and my mum and dad had it pumped into me never to go near there as it was extremely dangerous. Carlisle Circus had a number of Protestant churches namely St Enoch's, Clifton Street United, Carlisle Memorial and then there was the Orange Hall with the big statue of the Protestant leader on its roof. I had it pumped into my head that if I went up there I would be beat up by Protestants. Now I know there are non Catholic readers reading this but please remember that I was only five years old and this was real terror to me. I can honestly state that that is the reason why I'am a Commie today and free from these beliefs!

LIVING WITH THE ENEMY!

One good thing that we can state today is that the period that we have come to know as The Troubles is now behind us but today many of us can also look back at it and wonder how we survived. I myself grew up at the height of this period from the late 1960's and even though I had quite a few close shaves I am delighted to say that fate must have been on my side. One incident I can remember clearly is playing as a child with friends on the waste ground where part of the Westlink now stands and a gunman opening fire on us from Clifton Street and us running like mad to get away. All we were doing was playing with our Action Men and the person responsible must have known we were only kids but that did not stop him doing what he did. To us this was all very exciting and was a great big adventure but for our parents it must have been an out and out nightmare. Although generations of my family were brought up in an area known as the Fenian Gut I myself was brought up in Churchill House which is the New Lodge tower block next to the Westlink. When these blocks were built my dad got a job as a caretaker in Artillery Flats but was later moved to Churchill and had to take the caretakers flat which was on the ground floor next to the entrance. This was before the Troubles and one of my earliest memories is of my dad bringing me up on to the roof and seeing that the view was absolutely breathtaking - a view that still fascinates me to this day. But like everything else things were to change and a child growing up here things were to change a lot closer to home.

We all know that the conflict broke out in 1969 but it was not until two years later that things were to change for my family. On the 4th of May 1971 my dad was out on North Queen Street when he was grabbed by the British army and almost beat to death. So bad was this incident that images of it were broadcast throughout the world and the image of this occurring was to become one of the most famous of the Troubles. After medical treatment dad was thrown into jail and needless to say lost his caretaker job and looking back now as an adult this must have been hell for my mum but for me as a child I really had no idea what was going on and the adventure for us really began.

At around the same time I remember men digging up the road and erecting barricades. From talking to people years later I now know that these men were in fact the Official IRA and they were blocking off all the roads to stop the British Army coming into the area. One of these barricades was erected directly outside our flat and another early memory for me was how it was removed. One morning I remember being woke up by tremendous noise outside and looking out and seeing a tank removing this barricade.* Now it didn't have a cannongun on it and had a bull dozer section at the front but it was a bloody tank! Imagine being a kid looking out your window and seeing this thing driving past - now you can see why it was an adventure!

* It was said that these were only used in Derry. This one removed a barricade and then went down onto a carrier parked at the top of Great Georges Street

It's not everyday you get woke up by a tank outside your bedroom window!

Not long after this I remember being wakened by another tremendous noise and the whole block of flats in which we lived shaking. What happened this time was that the British Army decided to built a few observations posts on our roof and landed all the materials for doing so by helicopter. Quite a few runs were needed to do this and I can still remember the noise to this very day. The helicopters were to be frequent visitors whenever each army regiment tour ended and a new one began.

Once things settled down a bit we then sort of accepted our new roof top neighbours as something we could have fun with. In those days all of us had Action Men and these were our main plaything. My Action Man had all the gear and one of his outfits included a parachute. One of our daily adventures was to bring this Action Man up to the roof of the flats and getting the soldiers to throw it off for us. What normally happened was they would wait until we got down and lob it over and on quite a few occasions they let us out on to the roof to do it ourselves. This happened every other day and I can recall one incident where the soldiers were ending their tour and not wanting to leave any food for the next batch coming on they gave it all to us to bring home. This was all in military style cans (well it would be wouldn't it!) and the one memory I have here is the taste of the jam - it was beyond belief. This arrangement continued for some time and ended one day when we went up to throw our Action Man off. One of the soldiers let us in as normal but when we got up the stairs to the engine room where they all stayed there were about three soldiers on the far side of the room and when we went in they screamed their heads off to get us out. There was only two off us and at the time we were baffled as to why they wanted us out or what it was that we done wrong. The soldier bringing us down said something along the lines of "Sorry kids but that's the James Bond something or other." Needless to say we hadn't a bloody clue but today we know exactly who they were. Now for years the British Government stated that there was no SAS based on the roof of these high rise flats but if that's the case then who was it that shouted for us to get out and in the middle of all the graffiti left behind by the British troops why does it clearly say S.A.S. to this very day!

DADS INFAMY

Here's an interesting question. Throughout the whole period known as The Troubles what would you say is the single most famous photograph?

Would it be the well known picture of IRA hunger striker Bobby Sands or even the image of the priest waving a white handkerchief to seek help for one of those struck down during Bloody Sunday?

It may even be the picture of body parts being scraped up after Bloody Friday!

Sometimes the most simple picture can go on to become world famous and bearing this in mind (I know I'm going to be a bit biased) I think I can claim that one of the most well known images is not only a North Belfast picture, and indeed a New Lodge one, but I'll go one step further and claim that the extremely famous picture I'm talking about is of my Da!

Understandably there are many readers who are going to instantly dismiss this claim but before you do, allow me to present my case.

On the 4th of May, 1971, a major disturbance broke out in the New Lodge area following a number of incidents at the Gallaher Tobacco Factory at its North Queen Street end.

My Dad was the caretaker of the nearby flats and came out to see what was going on. At the same time members of the Royal Highland Fusiliers arrived and being one of the few men at the scene he was grabbed, severely beaten, thrown into the back of a military saracen, taken away, and lobbed into Crumlin Road Jail. Another group of people who arrived on the scene at the same time as the British Army were sections of the world's media and so, in a few short seconds, one of the most famous images of the Northern conflict was created.

Now I have pointed out that my Dad was never a political man and was one of the most respected people in the whole New Lodge area (I guess the opposite of me!) During the conflict he would often comment after a British soldier was killed that he and his family should be pitied.

While having a pint he often stated to me that if we lived in Manchester, Liverpool, Glasgow, Cardiff or London we would more than likely have ended up in the British Army only to end up dead in a place like this over a conflict we knew absolutely nothing about. But although my Dad was a very forgiving character the beating he got on that occasion must have left its mark because every time the Fusiliers were mentioned it was a good idea to get out of the way.

Not only that, but every time the Black Watch was mentioned a similar reaction was obtained. Now I don't have a clue if the Fusiliers and the Black Watch are the

same or if the both were involved in said incident but the forgiving nature was lost upon hearing the names of these regiments.

The basic image was my Dad being beaten by British soldiers and this was the picture which has appeared in dozens of books written on the Northern conflict, international magazines, posters and of course TV.

The whole incident was recorded on television and shown across the world. Those who drink in a well known New Lodge bar (which was his local) will be aware that the "Brit Thugs Out Now" poster was displayed behind the bar in a framed picture. The reason for this is due to the amount of bets my Dad won here due to the fact that he appeared in a well known American TV programme. His bet was that he was in an episode of Kojak even though he was never in America in his life.

Those taking him up thought they were on a sure thing until they discovered that Kojak walked into an Irish bar and what was on the wall of the bar? - You've guessed it!

On the subject of bars even I believe that fate has a way of controlling our lives. Dad was scooped, badly beaten and thrown into jail at the time of this famous image. We lived in Churchill Flats (Now renamed CuChuliann House) and guess what the nearest bar was?

Well for those not familiar with the area McGurk's was only yards away and have another guess where Dad's

watering hole was? So although he got a bad beating from the Scots in May 1971 it could have been worse. He could have been in his local on the 4th of December, 1971 but thankfully was in jail instead!

LE GOULAG BRITANNIQUE

RÉUNION - DÉBAT (avec projection d'un film)
AVEC DES REPUBLICAINS IRLANDAIS

à l'initiative du journal "IRLANDE LIBRE"

LET HE WHO IS WITHOUT SIN ...

All this now brings me up to the mid 1970's and here I was growing up in what was a war zone with a mother who was an alcoholic. Needless to say it was around this time that I began to 'go off the rails' a bit and find myself getting into constant trouble. Looking back I find this unsurprising as not only was I influenced by what was going on around me but also with what was being said. Marie Drum was the president of Sinn Fein and it was around this time that she made her famous speech of destroying Belfast brick by brick. On the wider scale there was also the music I was listening to which at that time was the Sex Pistols. So here I was listening to people wanting to destroy Belfast while at the same time listening to a punk group who wanted to destroy everything!

I took it literally. My fascination at the time was fire and I used to rush to the scenes of bombings and watch fires rip through the buildings so in time I developed a knack of doing it myself. It was also at this time that I was to change from primary school to secondary school but this was held up by a slight accident I had with a Joe loves fire, fire meets Joe's leg incident. I got burned on the lower section of my right leg and couldn't walk for nearly a year. What happened was we set fire to a pile of old plastic milk crates into which we threw an aerosol can. This exploded and sent a massive blob of

Sex Pistols

burning plastic onto my leg. The pain was unbearable. After being rushed to the nearby Mater Hospital I was detained there for quite some time for operations, painful skin grafts and physiotherapy. This was absolute hell and constant pain and you would've thought I would have learnt from it but unfortunately this was not the case.

Held up in school I had to do another year in primary before moving to St Patrick's Secondary School on the Antrim Road. If I hated primary school then I can only state that I utterly detested secondary school. With primary school I only had to walk down the street but with secondary school I had to walk down to York Street, get the No. 2 Ballyhenry bus and travel up the Antrim Road to a place I did not want to be. Looking back I know that the sensible thing to do would be to stay in school, study and pass exams but the fact of the matter was we were never given a chance. I hated all the teachers here and its hard to explain the circumstances but those I hated the most I later became really friendly with long after the school years. The class we were put in was known as C2 so that first year was 1C2, second year 2C2, etc. One of these teachers later told me that the C2 classes where simply for bums

I used to rush to the scenes of bombings and watch fires rip through the buildings

Clockwise - Owen Brophey (with closed eyes), Joe Moore, Joe Baker, Sean Collins and Colin O'Neill

on seats so that the school could get the money for them. They were given up on and no serious effort was to be made to teach them – This came from a former teacher and is not my view. Looking back I tend to agree because I can only think of one teacher who made an effort and that was big Brian 'Chuck' Connor. You have no idea how much I hated him but it's interesting how things turn around as, at the time of writing, I still visit him in a care home after he had a serious stroke some years ago. Now before you assume that I visit him so he must have been the one that told me all that stuff then no – I'm not that daft as it was another former teacher I'm friendly with.

It was also in secondary school where you met the gangs. Most where involved in what was called the Fianna which was the junior wing of the Provos. Because we lived in the Barrack area we were labelled either Sticks (Official IRA) or Erps (INLA). It was at this time that I had many run ins with the Fianna and in their quest to get me and give a good beating for being a bad boy they tried everything. In the end what they ended up doing was terrorising my mum and on one occasion I can remember up to twenty of them standing outside our flat waiting for me to come out. Needless to say when dad came home they all scampered as a lot of family on dad's side were involved in the Provo's and he would've went to any one of them. Looking back I can understand that I was a bit of a pain to the local community but I was more of a wee devil as some sort of an evil villain. However, also looking back, I often think of what became of these so called Fianna boys and the 'good citizens' they turned out to be!

There was the odd time that they did indeed catch me. On one of these I was taken to a house in Stratheden Street where I was forced to sign a statement saying I wrecked the local graveyard. Now I was surrounded by at least ten of these Fianna boys and naturally I was going to sign it. After I done so I was simply let go. This was strange and yes I did hang out in the local graveyard and did indeed commit acts of vandalism but it only consisted of pushing over the odd headstone but nothing serious.

In later years I discovered that this was to cover up more serious stuff of desecration on graves of which there were more serious acts of vandalism on what was termed 'Prod graves' and have a quick guess who was behind that! Not all of them I have to say but certain members.

On another occasion I was grabbed one night and taken to the local Incident Centre which was then on the New Lodge Road. This was for a house break in at Churchill House. In the incident centre I was beaten and with blood flowing from me taken to the nearby Sheridan Flats. Once there I was shown writing on the wall which said 'Kneecap Alley.' They asked me why do I think it was called 'Kneecap Alley' and my reply was "couldn't give a fuck." I was given another quick beating, tied to a lamp post and had a tin of paint poured over me. Now I'm sure that those brave Fianna members will confirm that my reaction was to shout "Provie bastards" because that is exactly what it was. As for the break in – that was committed by someone whose brother was high up in the local Provos!

Green Goddess

I may be giving the impression here of being anti IRA but I don't mean to. There were many people in my area who went on to become IRA volunteers and do the stuff that IRA volunteers do. I can not state that any of these people I'm referring to have ever done that. While others within the IRA were prepared to take on armed British soldiers, the chancers I am referring to were prepared to jump on their back and pick on local kids who were deemed trouble makers. I have words for it but cant state it in writing but it is centred around a global shape within the human anatomy and involves an obvious lack of it!

One thing I did not lack when growing up was the same global shape and this was something which was exploited by others who once again lacked the said shape. One of the first things which we were sent to do was go out and burn everything as this was a specialist talent. I think this was around 1977 and the fire brigade were on strike. Because of this the British army took over with their famous Green Goddess fire engines and we were sent out to burn anything that stayed still for two seconds. Now this is where is gets difficult because I can't remember what I was convicted for and what I got away with so I'm afraid I need to be quite general. One of the incidents I did get convicted for was one which I didn't do and that was the burning of the old Mission Hall in York Street.

I had been arrested by the Peelers (RUC) and they gave me a list of places recently burned down which they wanted to pin on me. Looking at the hand-written list I knew that I had done a few of them but not all of them.

The Peeler's had the advantage because here they were interviewing me without a parent, legal guardian or solicitor and doing so with me being twelve years of age. Looking back I cant imagine what my solicitor must have been thinking but Rumpole of the Bailey he obviously wasn't!

Bearing all this in mind there is one thing I really can tell you and be truthful. I was a professional arsonist and my nickname was The Firebug. I can assure you that I can reduce a building to a pile of rubble in less than an hour and while that is happening I can be at least twenty miles away securing an alibi. Now before you think that this involves some sort of high tech gear and an expertise in electronics then I can assure you that you are barking up the wrong tree.

I can do this with a candle, some petrol, a condom, some tissue and soap powder. I can also put together more sophisticated devices which includes batteries and watches, clocks or timers nicked from lamp posts but here's a question – how do I know this? Well the bottom line is - I was taught how to do it and the people who taught me how to do it sat in the local bars enjoying their wee drink while bloody prats like me went out and done their wee bit of dirty work.

Getting back to our new secondary school it was also known as Bearnagheeha (Irish for windy gap) but to us it was known simply as Barney. Today It's known as St Patrick's College and it is a brilliant education establishment but in those days it was quite different. If you could not fight then you were on to a loser and as none of us could fight we were doomed. One ticket out was if you had an older brother in the school but mine was in Park Lodge and about to leave so I was snookered to use the polite term. The first few weeks were hell but once you got to know the dodges then you got by. I was forced to wear a school uniform for the first time and I hated it. My mum loved it, in fact she even went one step further and got me the badge of the school and sewed it on to my blazer. This acted as a pick on me magnet and therefore ensured many a punch in the gob. Unlike primary school a bus had to be got to Barney and different groups of boys got their buses at different stops. As I said ours was on York Street close to the junction of Great George's Street and the advantage we had was that we were the first on so we had our choice of seats. It then went along York Street and up Duncairn Gardens and many a morning we were greeted with a brick thrown from the Protestant side but what I don't think they realised was that they were doing us a massive favour. Needless to say we could not continue on with the journey because we were so traumatised by the incident and once we got home all we stated was that the bus was attacked on Duncairn Gardens – we stretched the story a bit but we weren't telling any lies! Another past time about going to Barney was to work

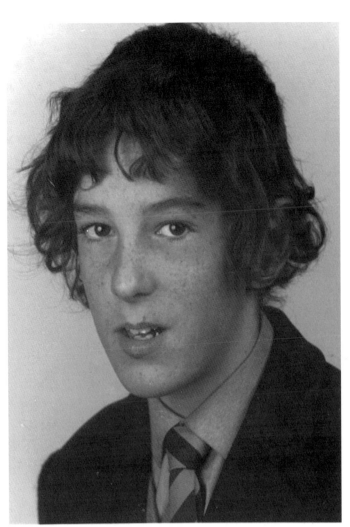

St Patrick's Secondary School (now college) The room below the 'x' was my first classroom in this school

out not going to it. There was bunking out and going on the hike. There were three things which always came together in Barney at least three of four times per week. Me, a form teacher and a leather strap. The first was always first thing on Monday morning because one habit we did develop was bunking out every Friday afternoon. It was nothing to do with getting away from school in general but getting away from P.E. as we hated it. Going on the hike was also a regular occurrence for us but looking back I think I would rather have been in school instead of walking about bored for six hours. One classic I remember was a few of the lads going on the hike and hiding their school bags in the bushes outside the City Hall. They were discovered but instead of parents being called it was the bomb squad. Barney boys in those days had military style school bags so obviously they were mistaken for bombs. One controlled explosion later and they were found out. I was no better. As previously stated on one occasion I thought that messing about on the ice in the Waterworks would be a better option than going to school. Some cracked ice, one frozen body and five days in intensive care soon proved that theory wrong.

I was only to stay in Barney for a couple of years as there was the slight matter of a few arson charges to be dealt with. Needless to say they were and I was sentenced to a training school order which was to St Patrick's on the Glen Road.

St. Patrick's Secondary School

Headmaster: W. J. STEELE, B.A., L.G.S.M., A.D.B.

Bearnageeha
Antrim Road
Belfast BT15 4DZ

Telephone: Belfast 770011/2/3

Dear Mr Baker,

Joe has been behaving badly at school. He has been late almost every morning since the start of the term. On Friday last I spoke to him and told him to stay in school all day but in spite of my warnings he left school without permission at lunchtime. Last term he left school without permission and almost got drowned in the Waterworks.

I would ask you to speak to him about this matter. If his behaviour continues to be like this, he is liable to find himself in serious trouble. If you wish to see me at anytime about Joe please do not hesitate to get in touch with me at the school. Yours sincerely. J. McGrath

One of many

Page 54

OFF TO THE HOUSE ON THE HILL

I don't remember my exact sentence to St Patrick's Training School but I think it may have been what was called 1 to 3 which meant you could do one year on good behaviour or three years on bad so you can guess which one I was set to do! I also don't remember the exact year but it was either 1978 or 1979 and although at the time of writing this was over thirty years ago I can remember that very first day as if it were yesterday.

At the courtroom I was taken out through a back door and placed in a holding cell. Then I was taken downstairs to another cell and locked up for a few hours. Today I look back at this and my detention in the North Queen Street Barracks and actually wonder if this was legal! Anyway when the door was opened I saw one of my childhood friends Dixie Dornan who was down from St Pat's for a remand hearing and I began to ask him what it was like. Needless to say Dixie obviously had the same twisted sense of humour as me and the description he gave me was obviously from something he saw in a war movie.

When we arrived at the Glen Road we turned into the grounds and went up this massive drive way with beautiful lawns and trees the whole way up. Then I saw the home for the first time and I can tell you it was certainly not what I expected. Because of Dornan's description I was looking for barbed wire fences, guard dogs and a building with tiny windows complete with bars. Instead I was met by a beautiful large building with the administration section in the centre and a chapel and gymnasium on either side of it and to the right the senior side and to the left the junior side. Needless to say I was to go to the junior side and my first night was spent in a large open dorm with about ten others in it. I don't think they came in that day as when I left the dorm they were still in it but what I do remember was that they were a bunch of cry-bas. Now don't get me wrong I was prone to the odd cry myself but not every bloody night!

A few days later I got my own room which was in the corridor next to the dorm. There were similar corridors upstairs and that was where I wanted to go but I guess that was not to be, but my pad was the furthest away from the house master's room so that suited me fine. I can't remember everyone who was in our corridor but next to me was Boo Gordon who lived in the Lisburn Road area. Boo was dead on and was a real fanatical fan of Led Zeppelin. Facing me was a guy called Beaver McCleave and all I remember about him was him arriving in one day with one of those tiny tv's which just came out then and all of us being fascinated by it. Today we would laugh at it but then it was real hi-tec! Next to him was 'E' Dixon who was also from the New Lodge area and the only other person in the corridor I remember was Paddy Gordon. Now if memory serves me right Paddy was from Downpatrick and for some unknown reason I took an instant dislike to him and sometimes went out of my way to make things hard for him. The first 'book' I ever helped with was with Boo Gordon and was called 101 Ways to Kill Paddy Gordon and although it may all seem humorous the bottom line is I was a bully and I'm sure Paddy must've really hated me. This being the case it was very rarely he had to put up with me as I was constantly hooking it (running away) from St Pat's.

A typical day began around 8am and it was up out of bed, showered and down for breakfast. After this we were lined up in the yard and then sent to our classrooms which were at the back of the building. The classrooms where what you would find in a normal school and the first teacher I ever got was a lady called Miss O'Rourke. She was one of the few teachers who actually took an interest in me and one of her aims was to teach me how to read and write which at that time was extremly basic for me. I could hardly write and when it came to reading I knew words but did not know what they meant. I was determined to do this and one of the things I was to do was borrow the Ladybird books, read them and then compare them to words in bigger books and in no time at all I was really learning very fast. One of the things Miss O'Rourke was to give me was a children's dictionary and when I went through that I was really begining to learn extremly fast. Another book I was given was a children's bible and once I read that I moved on to the bigger bible and it was from this that I began to take an intense interest in religion but not in the way the school had hoped. Mrs O'Rourke then tried me at writing and with joined up writing but that was one thing I could never get the hang of and to this day I write in block captials.

It was also here that I was being taught something I was never taught before and was a subject I took an instant fascination with – Irish history.

I was given a set of four books called The Living Past and these were the actual books from where my interest in Irish history began. We also read all the stories about CuChulann and the Children of Lir and I can state now that I simply couldn't get enough if it.

The other classes we did were arts and crafts and I really enjoyed these. These were taken by Brother John and we did everything from making nailboards right through to oil painting with knives which totally amazed me. Brother John was one of the nicest people you could ever meet and he really did enjoy teaching us kids everything he knew. Unfortunately there was also the one subject I absolutely detested and that was PE.

St Patrick's Training School on the Glen Road (Photograph Belfast Telegraph)

Never liked it, never have and never will. It was in St Pat's that my hurling career began and my hurling career ended. One day while doing this I received a direct hit in the face from a hurling ball and one burst mouth and several smashed teeth later I decided that I would never pick up a hurling stick again. However there was one other game we did play and I did enjoy that and became quite good at it and that was rounders. In America this is called softball and it was a game which I developed quite a talent for but there was no great demand for rounders players in Belfast at the time so I guess I was to go nowhere with that. Another PE event I did enjoy was swimming and St Pat's had their own swimming pool which I was in at every given opportunity but my main memory of it was the heating was never on but my preference was always for cold water swimming and when we went hiking in the nearby mountains then river swimming was something which we all really enjoyed. In St Pat's they also took us to other swimming pools such as at Andersonstown, Ballymena and our favourite, Lisburn. Lisburn had a massive diving platform which was brilliant to jump from as it was really high and it was this which kept us occupied for hours.

One thing that all new comers to St Pat's had to do was see the psychiatrist. I remember my visits to him and my thoughts were always that he was mad and not me. Because of what I was in for I was always called for an interview where I was constantly asked not only why I lit fires but why I burned buildings to the ground and my answer was always the same – the customary 'dunno.' He was also a bit weird as he would have asked how many times per day you masturbated. Now here's a grown man asking you how many times you serviced yourself – you're going to admit it like! He also showed the famous black cards with the smudges on them and asked you what you could see. Card 1 – blob. Card 2 – another blob. Card 3 – I don't believe it, it's another blob. He never liked these answers so I used to look again and say cat, dog, cow, hamster, elephant and he would write the answers down. What he ever made of them I don't know but before you think I'm some sort of serial killer then don't panic as I only made them up. My original answers of blob were the true ones.

Then came the day that one of my answers entered the volumes of urban legend only this one was true. One day he put a snooker ball on the desk in front of me and said that it was an apple and for me to eat it. I looked at the 'apple' and then at him and simply replied "You peel it and I'll eat it." Quite an answer for a kid but you need to understand how street wise and sarcastic I was at the time.

Another subject relating to St Pat's was all this stuff about pervy religious orders. The order that was in St Pat's was the De La Salle Brothers and I can state that 99.9% of them were fine and really committed to helping the kids in the home. There was only one whom we avoided like the plague as he was indeed a bit iffy. It was said that he used to do a bit of feeling up but to be honest I can not say if he did anything more serious. A few years ago there was an investigation into this sort of stuff at St Patrick's Training School but to be honest I can state that I had never heard anything about any of the Brothers but what I can state is that there were a few of the housemasters who were just a little bit over friendly but it never happened to me and I really can honestly state that. The Brothers were very strict and were not shy when it came to a good boot in the arse or slap across the head but that was it in relation to me.

There was also the family visits and I was visited quite regularly by mum and dad and my brother Liam. Liam always got me into bloody trouble as every time he came up he came on his motorbike and on his way out decided to have a quick scramble across the lawn. Have a guess who got the boot in the arse or slap across the head every time this happened!

It was also during one of these visits that I received absolutely dreadful news about one of my friends. Like all kids we thought we were going to live forever and that dying was for old people. Dad came up to see me one time during the day which was extremely unusual as all visits were in the evening and daytime visits only at the weekends. I was taken out of class and down to see my dad. When I went in he was totally silent and I knew right away that something was wrong.

Jim Madden

At first I thought it was to do with mum. As previously mentioned mum had a drink problem and shortly before I went into St Pat's she was in hospital for major surgery. She had bits of kidney, liver and spleen removed as well as other bits and bobs. She had been given the last rites several times but by some miracle she was to pull through and live for quite a few years. What dad told me was totally unexpected, sudden and absolutely heartbreaking and I can still hear the words to this day. "Your wee mate Jim Madden has been killed." I immediately burst out crying and then asked what had happened. He had been going to school and was messing around when he tripped – right under the wheel of a bus. He lived in number 12 of our flats and Jim and I had drifted apart when I began to be a really bad boy but he was one of my closest friends and going by the fact that all of the old Churchill House boys are still friends today I know that he would certainly have been one of them.

The following day I was to do something that I had never done before and that was to write a letter to his granny. Jim and his sister Karen lived with their granny and in this letter I told her how sorry I was but to be honest that's all I remember but I do know that she treasured this letter and later told me that it was one of the most heartfelt sympathies she had received.

On the day of Jim's funeral I spent it in the chapel of St Pat's. This was not due to any religious conversion but due to the simple fact that it was the quietest place in the whole building. I remember asking the question that I assume everyone has asked and that was the why has God allowed this to happen. I also remember looking at the large image of Jesus nailed to the crucifix and thinking that if he could allow this to happen to his son then what else would he be prepared to do! Don't think that this anti religious attitude came about at this time as it did not. I detested the fact that I made my First Holy Communion and at my Confirmation I point blankly refused to kiss the Bishops ring but in fairness someone else's runny, snattery nose had more to do with this than the beginning of a religious rebellion.

As I have said my interest in religion began in St Pat's and there was also a voluntary class which anyone could attend every Wednesday night and that was a religious one. The only people I remember attending this was the previously mentioned Paddy Gordon and a guy called McCambridge who had a desire to become part of one of the religious orders. This was a type of theological class and was with a priest. I had a bible and I would spend the week going through it and looking for the usual contradictory stuff to put to the priest and looking back now he must've really hated me. I would go through the bible and take notes and then present them to the said priest but I never focused on the usual incest or eye for an eye and then forgiveness rubbish but would look at the more complex stuff. For example I would concentrate on good versus evil complexes. On one occasion my argument was as follows:- At God's right hand was the Arch Angel Lucifer and he was cast out of heaven with

Quite often I caught the priest out with questions on why God's most trusted angel Lucifer turned against him. All I ever got was "mystery of the faith my son!"

angels which numbered the grains of sand in the desert. Now to me this was God's most trusted servant and one hell of a lot of angels and when I had the priest caught out what was his reply? "That's a mystery of the faith my son!" I hated that answer as to me it was simply a way of covering their back but to be honest I knew that I had them. What soon developed was a priest on one side stating that Roman Catholicism was the one true faith and me on the other with my argument that it was all a load of superstitious nonsense. What is interesting is that when the said priest retired the one person he wanted to see was not the altar licking McCambridge but me. I remember his exact words to me and they concluded by him saying "Young Baker if there was no Protestant religion you would invent it." To this day I don't know if that was an insult or a compliment.

St Pat's was indeed a very religious institution and I was certainly to leave my mark on their chapel in a humourous way as I will explain later but sadly there were other incidents which were more dramatic and which I stuck with tradition and got the blame for.

One night we were all woken from our beds and moved to the far side of the building. There was a fire and the fire was in the chapel. Now here was me with my openly expressed hatred of the Catholic Church and a conviction of arson so who do you think was going to get the blame? The following morning two house masters stood at either side of me as I was getting washed. They were two of the ones I liked and became close too and were Jim Whinnery and Tommy Mahon. They asked me about the fire and I replied by asking them a simple question. "Is the building still

standing?" "Yes" they replied. "Then it obviously wasn't me then." I don't know what their conclusion was but I think they believed me as I was never interviewed by the Peelers (police).

Later I was asked did I know who did it and I said no but the fact of the matter is I did. The person who did it was one hell of a twisted individual whom was operating outside as a homosexual rent boy but before anyone considers opening up a new investigation I totally forget his name and description – after all it was over thirty years ago!

However, I believe, this chapel fire was to seal my fate in relation to St Pat's. I had a reputation of fear in this place that led my fellow tenants to be absolutely terrified of me. For some unknown reason those who seemed to pick on me developed this knack to encounter some sort of strange accident. For example there were some who switched on their bedroom lights only to discover the dangers of electricity as it shot down their arm as someone had interfered with their light switch. There were others who had developed strange cigarette type burns on the backs of their necks or worse still deep inside their ear but as I hinted at previously this was sheer coincidence and nothing to do with me! To give another idea of this fear there was one person I got into a number of fights with. Unfortunately for me this person was a better digger (fighter) than me and continuously showed me up on each of our encounters. My solution was simple. To stab him. One night I sneaked out of my room and broke into the kitchens. There I stole two knives and my plan was really to cause serious damage to this rival. Needless to say the missing knives were reported the following morning and were found inside my mattress. I had told only one person of my plan and although I thought him an obvious scumbag at the time I really am glad that he did what he did as I think I might've got myself into a bit of serious trouble if I had gone though with my plans. My main rival (whom I planned to stab) and I became friends and I think that this was more due to him being told of the sort of threat that he was under from me.

The reason I am pointing this out is certainly not to make me out to be some sort of Belfast 'Kray Twin' but to give you an idea of what was to happen to me was totally unexpected and the only way I can describe the events would be for you to imagine Barbie taking on Darth Vador!

I can only state what I knew at the time but if it is fact I can not say. There was a fellow inmate called Charlie Monaghan and I has always assumed that Charlie was one of the orphans placed in St Pat's. That's all I knew about him.

One day we were out in our usual line up in the yard to go to our class rooms when totally out of the blue Charlie kicked me on the back of the leg. It bloody hurt and my instant reaction was to turn round and hit him a massive punch in the face. Suddenly one of the house masters grabbed me by the back of the hair and ran me straight into a pebbledash wall. Now for legal reasons allow me to explain this as though I were giving a statement. I was tightly grabbed by the back of my long hair by a house master, whom I assumed was there for my care and well being, and my face pushed forcibly into a pebbledash wall. Now you may be surprised to learn that my face was turned into a bloody mash and that to this day I have several scars on my chin, eyes, cheek and still have to receive hospital treatment for bleeding noses but I was sent to the headmaster. Now in fairness to the said house master he had a desire for me to go and clean myself up but strangely this was something I refused to do.

I was left sitting outside the headmasters office and it was then that I decided to take matters into my own hands and that was to go for Charlie Monaghan.

He was in the same class as me and was therefore at Brother John's arts and crafts class. This was a class he was never to forget.

I stormed up the stairs and straight into the class. I then snapped a heavy 'T' ruler off the blackboard and used it to give Charlie Monaghan the most violent and bloody beating he was ever likely to receive.

When I was finished I simply went back down to my spot outside the headmasters room to await my fate.

The headmaster never had the nerve to face me and soon after, two men came up the corridor, put me in handcuffs and took me to a waiting car which was outside.

Now this occurred thirty years ago and one would think that it is all long in the past and has no effect on today. It does. I have no plans to go back into prison but there is a chance that it will happen. The house master who did this to me was a grown man and I was a child. Things have now changed and I am now a grown man. If I ever bump into the said house master I will give him more of a chance than he ever gave me. I will give him the opportunity to again smash my face into a wall and see how things develop this time.

Aerial photograph showing part of North and West Belfast.
1 - Part of the Barrack area. 2 - Clifton Street Cemetery. 3 - Unity Flats. 4 - Shankill Estate.
5 - Belfast Prison (The Crum). 6 - Ardoyne

629/80 HUMAN SCUM

On leaving St Pat's in the company of the people I was handcuffed to I was asked question after question as to what happened to me. I told them and they're reply was that I must have deserved it but even I could tell that these two men were shocked at the extent of the injuries to my face. Another weird question was if I was in the IRA? No was my reply but later it struck me that this was one hell of a pretty stupid question because even if you were you were hardly going to turn round and say yes! I had absolutely no idea where I was going but soon found out - Hydebank Young Offenders Centre. On my arrival I was taken to reception and the screw on duty took one look at me and sent me instantly to the prison hospital. Here I was treated and cleaned up and then sent back to reception. On my arrival back I was told to strip and handed a very short towel to cover myself. This all occurred in a tiny cubical and when ready, I was taken out, had my hair cut and given a bath. Now when I say a bath it was about three inches of water and I have no idea what I was given to clean myself with but if it was soap then it must've been the cheapest most useless stuff they could get their hands on!

On getting out of my bath I was told to put my towel on and move to another section. Here I was measured, weighed and notes taken of tattoos and scars. I was then handed a uniform which was dark blue trousers and light coat and a light blue shirt. This was crap but to make matters worse I was given the brightest red jumper you could imagine and told to wear it. God did I feel like a right dick! A screw then came to me and I can still remember clearly his exact words to me which were. Your number is 629/80 and you are nothing but a piece of human scum. I was then taken to Elm Wing and to the Junior Remand Unit where I was to spend the next five weeks after which I was to have been returned to St Pat's. On my first night I got a visit from one of the screws. When I came on to the wing I had it drummed into me what you were to do when a screw came in to your cell and that was to jump to your feet and state your number, name and sentence which in my case was remand. This I did not do so the screw grabbed my by the throat and pushed me against the bars of the window and pushed his face into mine and said "my name is Billy. Billy the Bastard and you are not to fuck with me." Mistake number one – I burst out laughing. I soon got the hang of doing what I was told and the following morning my routine was to begin. I was woke with the banging of the cell doors around 7am but my door was not banged. I got up anyway and made my bed and got ready as that was all I could remember what to do. About half an hour later a screw came to my door and shouted through "Baker you are to stay in your bed." Apparently the doctor who treated me the day before had instructed that I was to rest for a few days because I had lost a bit of blood – well somebody could've told me! Back to bed I went but I was already wide awake. It made no difference anyway as I became a bit of a freak show as every chance they got the prisoners were lifting the flap of my cell door and looking in. "What are you in for?" they continuously asked. I didn't know exactly but couldn't resist saying "killing three hundred chickens." We all know how Chinese whispers work and around an hour later another prisoner would come to my door ask ask "are you in for killing five hundred chickens?" "Yep" was my simple reply and away they would go. The following day I was still in bed and still getting my door flap visitors. "What the fuck did you kill a thousand chickens for?" they would ask. "Hate the fuckers" would be my reply" and away they would go to discuss the crimes of their new wing mate.

Unknown to me outside the cell was a card on the wall which stated my number, name, religion and sentence. Later the second day the flap on my door went up and one of the prisoners shouted in "Is that you Joe? (He didn't recognise me with the short hair as I always had it long) "Aye, who's that?" was my reply. "You'll find out when you get out of your cell." I was bloody raging as I didn't know who it was but I did find out later that it was someone I knew from Unity Flats. Later that night he came to my cell door, opened the flap and shouted in "What the fuck are you doing telling people you're in for killing chickens for?" Apparently he went back to association and put the record straight but it was a laugh while it lasted.

The following day the same prisoner was allowed into my cell to show me the ropes in terms of cell cleaning and making bedpacks. Now Hydebank today is a bit of a holiday complex but then it was more like a military camp and run along military lines. Now you need to understand that this was thirty years ago (1980) so I will try to give as best an idea of daily routine as I possibly can but understand that there may be a few details that I may have forgot about.

Wakey wakey time was around 7am when the screws came onto the wing and banged the doors with the stupid saying of "Hands off cocks and on socks." Now I know they must've thought that they were pretty cool coming down with their wee vulgar statement but we just though they were a bunch of wankers. When the screws came down screaming "get out of bed you wee bastards" then they were the ones we jumped straight out of bed for.

H. M. PRISON
&
YOUNG OFFENDERS CENTRE
HYDEBANK WOOD

Now your toilet and sink was in the cell so first you did what came naturally in the morning and then washed and shaved at the sink. Shaving was out for me as this was not to come for a few years later but washed I did do. You then had to make up your bedpack which was a military style folding of your sheets and blankets which were placed at the top of your bed. At the bottom was your small towel on which was placed your razor (without blade as this was handed into you soon after wake up and taken back again), shaving brush, toothbrush, toothpaste and soap. At the bottom of your bed stand was your big towel which had to be wrapped around perfect and as tight as a drum. You then had to clean your cell and when I say clean I mean clean. Random inspections would be carried out and a white cloth would be wiped across your floor and if there was a tiny speck of dust on it you were in deep shit. On being let out of your cell you then had to clean the wing and then breakfast. Now when I say breakfast I mean a tiny drop of Cornflakes or porridge, even less milk and a round of toast which was made about three hours previously. On this you had an extremely tiny bit of margarine and a mug of absolutely stinking tea with no sugar and served in a massive plastic mug.

After so called breakfast it was off to the education block and to school. It was here that I met a lady called Mrs Durey and she was, for some unknown reason, to take an interest in my education. I told her the stuff I was reading in St Pat's and she went and got me it. This included the Irish history books and looking back I really must say that this woman went out of her way for me. What's more interesting was the fact that although she was getting me Irish history books she was in fact a staunch Unionist and made no secret of this fact. A few years later I met her and it was in the most unlikely places (well for me anyway!) During the Ulster Says No rallies of the mid 1980's a few mates from Hydebank days had organised a brilliant scam to make money. What they did was went down to some band shop in Sandy Row and picked up a few Ulster Says No posters and then to another shop and got a few buckets. Back in their pad in Divis Flats they stuck the posters onto the buckets and went down to the Loyalist protests at the City Hall and walked among the crowd rattling the buckets as an Ulster Says No collection. They wanted me to do it but one day I went down to suss it out and who did I bump into in the middle of all these thousands of Loyalists? Dear old Mrs Durey. Now she knew I was a Catholic from the New Lodge and if she had said the wrong thing then I could have been savagely kicked to death but she just looked at me and said "Hello Joe, nice to see you here." That was my first and last visit down to one of these rallies. My Divis Flats friends were lifting an average of seven hundred quid per rally and there was me, among quarter of a million Prods bumping into the only bloody Protestant I knew!

Anyway back to Hydebank and the schooling of Mrs Durey. If there was one person who wanted to see me read and write then it would have been her. At that time she was pretty old and I suspect she is now dead but now that I have written over two hundred publications and write for numerous newspapers there is only one person that I would love to know about and that is her.

School was only in the mornings and at dinner time we were taken back to the wings and to the canteen for our din dins. Now dinner is a loose term here as if you thought breakfast was bad then dinner was worse. This usually consisted of meat and two veg in minimal portions and followed by a desert which was just as bad and which I always remembered was what we called frog spawn. I had the advantage here as I loved the stuff and I would often get several portions. I also had the same advantage on liver days as no one could stand the stuff but I bloody loved it and once again obtained several portions. Friday was the same as that was Fenian Steak day which was fish. A lot of the Prods refused to touch it as they saw it as some sort of Catholic religious feast and in Hydebank it was as they didn't take it and all us Catholic's did indeed have a feast with their share of the fish!

After dinner we were locked up for an hour to allow the screws to get a drink at the POA bar within the complex (serious!) On being let out it was then workshop time and my choice was painting and decorating. Now I can't remember the name of our tutor but the name Stewarty springs to mind. Here we were taught everything there is to know about painting and decorating and I absolutely loved it. I was taught everything from the difference to matt, gloss and egg-shell paint right through to sign writing and do you know I remember it all to this day.

After training it was back up to the wing again and this time it was for supper and although I can remember everything about breakfast and dinner I can not remember a single supper so I'm afraid someone is going to have to drop me an e-mail and remind me what we got for this!

When whatever we got was complete we were locked up for another hour and the screws allowed their second drink. Now during these lock ups the screws went to what we termed the Prison Officers Association Club which was within Hydebank and every time they came back they smelt of drink. Now I know it was not all the screws but that was our impression of what went on during our lock-up.

Night time we were allowed out for a few hours association and that was into the canteen area. There was two small rooms of the canteen and one was a TV room and the other was a games room. The TV room had a black and white TV in it and the only time I

remember it being watched by everyone was for Top of the Pops on Thursday night. The games room is where I spent most of my time and the only games available were chess and draughts. Now chess I'm pretty good at but players will know that you need a lot of concentration and you were never going to get that in the games room of a young offenders centre. Draughts was a different matter and this is a skill that must be in the blood as Granda Baker was a bit of an expert. There is a technique of two moves and once these two moves are made then you are unbeatable. Today I have downloaded this game on my iPhone and the computer is even yet to beat me. Anyway I know I'm showing off but the point I'm making is that this came in useful for winning all sorts and because I didn't smoke at the time then fruit shortcakes was my constant prize. Another racket I developed was ironing and in Hydebank when you got your clothes back from the laundry you had to iron them yourself. This was something I had a knack for and something that earned me more than enough packets of shortcake biscuits. In the main canteen area there were tables where you just sat around and talked and there was also a dart board at the far end of the room. Outside of the games room I enjoyed sitting around having a chat so it was at these tables that I could mostly be found. Those I was in with totally fascinated me and, apart from a childhood friend, this was the first time I had ever met Prods.

Before anyone accuses me of being sectarian because I use the term Prod then lets just face up to reality for a few moments. On the Unionist/Loyalist side people are known as Prods, Huns and Orangies. On the Catholic/Nationalist side they are known as Fenians and Taigs and the two most common terms are Prods and Fenians and people from my generation and beyond on both sides will totally agree with me. Anyway the first Prod I ever sat down with was a guy called Rab Skey from the Loyalist Suffolk area in West Belfast. I really liked Rab and the both of us were really friendly during my few weeks in the Junior Remand Unit. Life in the Junior Remand Unit was bloody hell but I knew I was only to stick it out for few weeks before going back to St Pat's where I had planned to bloody behave from now on. On my final day I was taken from the Junior Remand Wing and said my good-byes to everyone and the unique thing here was that I liked everyone on our wing. Now in fairness it was a pretty small wing but I can honestly state that everyone was sound. That morning I was to learn that my new found friend Rab Skey was to also go for a court hearing. Now I know what people are thinking and that is that if I were so close to him and was talking to him then I would've known about his hearing. That would be true but Rab's court hearing was brought forward and the first he heard about it was that morning. I can't remember exactly, but Rab was for a hearing from Rathgale (the Protestant training school) and my hearing was from St Pat's. What was to happen next was to shock both of us.

When you misbehaved in St. Pat's you were usually sent to Hydebank for the short sharp shock treatment and then returned to the training school. If I can remember right there was never a case of a permanent Hydebank stay but if there was going to be a first then it just had to be bloody me.

When I went into court I was expecting a telling off and sent back to the home. Instead what I was told was that I was going to Hydebank for almost two years. Now today if you were to ask me what I was sentenced for I couldn't tell you but I'm sure it was for something. If it was for a crime of say beating Charlie Monaghan half to death then why was I never interviewed in a peeler barrack? Bear in mind that although it was a young offenders centre it was in fact a prison sentence. Now my solicitor of the time (the same Rumpole mentioned earlier) never saw me until this court appearance. Why did he not look into what was going on? My view today is down to my injuries and the brutal assault of the so called house master. No mention was made in court of his horrific assault on me or of the injuries I received. Looking back I think that if I had had a half decent solicitor at the time things would have been so different and I would be worth quite a few thousand quid due to my inflicted injuries but I'm sure most of it would've been lost as I would've had to pay it to poor Charlie!

In the same court Rab was told a similar story and his reaction was the same as mine – to burst out crying. I have no shame in stating that I cried. Here I was, as a child, being told I was sentenced to almost two years in prison. If that was bad then worse was to come. In the cell behind the court my Mum was allowed in to see me. When she seen me crying she also bust into tears. Back at St Pat's there were very few house masters that I liked but there was one whom I was very friendly with and if ever the term two faced scumbag ever applied to anyone then it was him. In the back courtroom he turned to my crying mum and said "Mrs Baker, get used to it because you'll not be seeing your son for a few years."

On being taken from this back room I was handcuffed and taken downstairs. When going along the downstairs corridor my mum was ahead of us crying her eyes out. The screw I was handcuffed to showed respect and kept me well behind until she turned out in the main gallery of the courtroom. As for me I was taken to Townhall Street, thrown into the cells and then taken back to Hydebank to begin my sentence.

On being sentenced to Hydebank I can honestly state that I was in shock. I was taken to the wing below the Junior Remand Unit which was called Elm House (all the wings were named after trees) and placed in a cell for lock up. There were various ways of communicating from cell to cell and the most common one was via the heating pipes. These are large pipes which ran across the back of the cell and which ran the length of the whole block. Because heating pipes expand when warm and contract when cold this resulted in small gaps from cell to cell. When locked up I prepared my cell which meant getting my bedpack ready and having the cell spotless. Suddenly I heard the rapping of the pipes which was a sort of morse code and went down to the side in which the rapping was coming from. "Is that you Joe?" was whispered. "Yes" I replied. It was Rab who was placed in the next cell. "What happened?" he asked, "thought you were going back to St Pat's?" he added before I could answer. Holding back the tears I told him what had happened that day and then he told me his similar story. Then he asked "do you want a smoke in?" I said yes.

This was the beginning of my smoking career as the shock of my sentence had drove me to it and then we began what was called 'passing'. This was the means of passing one item from cell to cell and could be done through the gaps in the pipes, under the doors using string taken from the blankets or from window to window using the same string. Because I needed the cigarette to be lit we decided to use the window method. Rab passed me in a cigarette and I then sat down and had my first smoke which I thought was disgusting, smelly and totally tasteless. However, this being the case, he offered me one about an hour or two later and again I said yes. This time the cigarette never made it as one of the screws had been listening to our chat in the corridor. As soon as Rab was passing the screw banged his door and immediately put us both on report. The following day we were taken up before the governor and he decided to come down heavy on us both. We were sentenced to three days on the boards and a loss to two weeks remission. This was two weeks on our sentence which basically meant that we had been sentenced of two weeks in jail for passing a bloody cigarette! There are people who do less time in prison for refusing to pay fines of hundreds of pounds! The boards were another experience. This was solitary confinement and the reason it was called the boards was because that's what your bed was – a board bolted to the ground. My favourite bit was the fact that they even had a pillow shaped solid bit of wood to rest your weary head on! Also in the room was a plastic gallon container of luke warm water, a bible and a piss pot and that was it. There was a window but it was a thin shaped opening at the top of the wall beyond reach and was closed off with sanded perspex which meant that you couldn't see out even if you could reach it. This was home for twenty three hours a day and for one hour you were allowed out into the exercise yard, alone, to walk around in a circle in an enclosed yard which took you 132 steps to walk around it.

This was a place I was to get used to because I was to go back quite regularly and as for my remission – well I kissed most of that good-bye!

To be honest most of the screws were ok and there was one with whom I got very friendly with. His hobby was model railways. These had always fascinated me and I would've sat mesmerised as he told me about his collection and how it all worked. He knew I was genuine and he would often bring me in books on the subject which I always read intensely. The only other screw I remember was the PE teacher who was an English man named Hardy. Now his story was always that he was in the Parachute Regiment and that he was there on Bloody Sunday. I believed it at the time but looking back I think he may have been spoofing.

Hardy was tiny and I'm no expert on the Para's but my guess would be that they don't take midgets! Mr Hardy may have been small but I can confirm he was bloody tough! His idea of PE was exactly the same as what it would be for the army and that was bloody murder. Push ups, sit up, run, squat, run again, turn, run, sit ups – I can still hear it all in my head. You know how in school for PE they would take you outside on good days. Well Mr Hardy was the opposite. On good, cold rainy days we were taken to the playing fields at the back of the prison and here we 'played' a game which was quite

unique to say the least. Before we went out we had to put on gym gear which was about to be thrown out in the bin and were instructed to tie our track shoes on very tightly. We then went to the back field and a medicine ball was placed in the centre of it. Now for those who don't know a medicine ball is a big leather ball which weighs a bleeden ton and which is used in gyms for various things.

On this occasion it was used for creating a murder match. When the ball was placed in the centre of the pitch we were divided into two teams who had to line up at each end of the pitch. Now there are many ways to divide teams such as even numbers and odd numbers or even getting two 'captains' to pick their own teams but this was totally unknown to Mr Hardy. His method was quite simple – Fenians and Prods or for those not in the know – Catholics and Protestants. The purpose of the game was to get the heavy medicine ball back to your own goal for a point and the only rule – no spitting!

It was always a bloody murder match and no matter how many times I tried to lie low I always got some (insert word to doubt someone's parentage) who threw the bloody medicine ball to me. By some miracle I managed to get it back to our goal and secure a point but unfortunately it was to be a bit of a regrettable incident. The Prods were beaten by one point and one of them, a giant (well he was big to me) called Ozo grabbed me and told me in no uncertain terms that he was going to beat the **** out of me later. I assumed this was going to happen back in the showers but fortunately (for me at the time) a massive fight broke out in the showers and yours truly managed to avoid all this by taking slightly longer than usual at the toilet.

The threat from Ozo was not forgot about. He later got me up in the ablutions (washing area) and gave me a headbutt which sent me flying across the room. I know this may sound strange but that was it. There was no deep down animosity and when you got your bashing it did not go on and on like a play ground bully and to be honest I'm glad it didn't. Now I know Ozo's second name but I don't want to state it in case I'm mistaken but I think this guy was in for bloody murder so try and imagine how my life would have been if he had decided that I was to be his subject of bullying! This was not to be. There was another guy inside who was equally as mad only he was a Taig. Him and Ozo detested each other but Ozo had met his match and those two were more worried about keeping an eye on each other than to worry about someone like me.

Anyway getting back to the screws and there was another I remember very, very well. For the purpose of this I will call him Nixon. Nixon had it in for me and even to this day I find it very hard to believe why. One day he came into my cell and after all the formalities of standing to attention, shouting out my name, number and sentence he grabbed me and threw me against the wall. He then asked me who my da was and I told him "Charlie Baker" to which he grabbed me by the throat. He then went on to slap me about a bit and inform me that he and so and so Baker of the Shankill Orange Hall were such and such. Now I can't remember exactly what he said but my understanding was that he and someone called Baker had a bit of a fall out in the

Shankill Orange Hall and he had assumed it was my da. Now credit where credit is due I understand our family is originally from the Shankill area but we had sort of changed sides some years previously and all Nixon had to do was look at my cell card. This card went everywhere with you and was placed outside your cell and on it was your number, name, religion, sentence date, short release date (with full remission) and long release date (with loss or remission). Now all Mr Nixon had to do was go to the said cell card, look at the section which stated religion and then work out how many Roman Catholic's were likely to show up at the Shankill Orange Hall!

What was normal then was that you worked yourself from house to house (wings) and my next stop was Willow and then over to Beech. When in Elm and Willow you had your own toilet and sink in your cell but when over at Beech you had none as you could leave your cell and go to the toilet at the end of the wing which was some sort of reward for good behaviour. My move had nothing to do with good behaviour as it was at this time that Borstal had closed down and the prisoners moved to Hydebank. The cells in Willow had bunkbeds placed inside them and the prisoners from Borstal placed in them with everyone else. I had been doubled up with a prisoner from Unity Flats and both

Hydebank Young Offenders Centre ©Google

of us absolutely hated each other. To say that we constantly fought would be an understatement but one night his bed mysteriously caught fire and that was my ticket out. I got moved to Beech and he got moved to the boards for smoking in bed. Did I set him up? Yes is the straight forward and honest answer.

Over in Beech life was not to get any easier. It was at this time that the Hunger Strike was on in the H Blocks (above). There were daily arguments between prisoners and sometimes these got a bit heated. As a result of the first hunger strike our uniform was to change. What we had was dark blue trousers and coat with a light blue shirt. We then got trousers, shirts and jumpers which were meant to be civilian style but which looked more like something out of an Action Man kit. Needless to say the IRA prisoners back at the H Blocks were not happy about this and as a result they embarked on a second hunger strike. Now I know the second hunger strike was not only related to the uniform issue but it was part of it. On our wings every aspect of the hunger strike was argued and many fights did indeed break out. Prison officers were gunned down by the IRA and INLA and when this occurred everyone was locked up and we didn't even get our hours exercise.

At the time of the second hunger strike we didn't expect anyone to die. I remember us being taken to the education block and shown booklets which portrayed life in Northern Ireland prisons as being comfortable. It was then that I was being informed that prisoners in the H Blocks were locked up constantly and that they were on dirty protests which meant they had to spread their excrement etc. on the walls. This was all news to me and of course I took a deep interest in it all but where

do you think I was hearing all about this?

It is true that a lot was coming from fellow prisoners but it was actually a screw that was telling me what it was all about! Now I can't say his name as I'm sure he is still alive but if he is reading this then all I can say that he was one of the biggest influences in my life. He informed me of the whole political situation and why republican and loyalist prisoners were different. It was he who told me that if it were not for the situation in Northern Ireland most of these prisoners would be leading normal everyday lives. Now for the shock. Many reading this will assume that this would be coming from some sort of lefty, liberal screw but you would be totally wrong. This was coming from a screw who was as loyalist as loyalist could be and who was as anti IRA as you could get.

But then the unthinkable happened. On the 5th of May 1981 Bobby Sands died on hunger strike. To be honest I think it was a shock to everyone including the loyalists who believed that the strikers would never see it through. I can remember quite a few of these prisoners stating that they hoped he was burning in hell but when you talked to them one on one over a chess game or darts they stated how they admired them for what they had done and were doing. This was something that was new to me because I could never imagine doing what these hunger strikers did and I have no shame in stating that they must surely be among the bravest people that have ever walked on this planet. Now I know I have only mentioned the first, Bobby Sands, but nine other republican prisoners from the IRA and INLA followed him and it was from this that my interest in republican politics began.

When the hunger strike in the H Blocks concluded everything began to settle down. In Hydebank I can't remember exactly what the situation was in relation to wearing your own clothes but I think I can remember that you had to wear the civilian style uniform during the day and your own clothes in the evening at association and at the weekends. As soon as I became a sentenced prisoner I got to do half day work and half day education. In the morning it was the usual routine of up with the roosters, washed, cell and wing cleaned and then breakfast. For me it was off to the education block but don't be thinking that this was out of choice as I was still under 16 and had to go to school. Saying that I really enjoyed it and some of the teachers in there were really committed to educating us young riff raff. As previously mentioned Ms Durey really helped me along and one of the things she encouraged in me was poetry. I didn't realise it but I was very good at this (still am) and Ms Durey must have really enjoyed them because I remember writing one and when she read it she snapped at me. Strangely it is the only poem I remember to this day.

As I awoke one morning
To the early joys of spring
There upon my window sill
So sweetly did it sing
A little robin red breast
His breast was ohh so red
So I gently closed my window
And crushed the ******** head

Well I thought it was good! This was the only time Ms Purdy cracked up at me so everything else must've been impressive. It was also at this time that I went back to reading the dictionary and making sense of the words I was hearing every day. I also began to read the bible again and with the amount of time I was on the boards with nothing else sometimes this was a forced choice. If I was confused in St Pat's with this book then that was intensified. Reading the book of Revelation and being informed that the world was going to end and then quoting the prayer Our Father where it is stated that 'thy will be done on earth as it is in heaven.' Am hello - is the world not going to end. Anyway I think I got a bit too much into it. Having read the bible about four or five times I can tell you this for a fact. You can read whatever you want into it and there are quotes and passages throughout it with which anybody can make up their own religion. Just look at all those pay to pray nuts in America and you'll understand what I'm talking about.

It was also in Ms Durey's class that a major change was to overcome me and stay with me right up to this very day. One day we were doing the history of the

Soviet Union when I came across a picture in a book, a picture which was to have a massive impact. The book was called *Portrait of Moscow* and inside was a photograph of a statue called the worker and collective farmer. (Above) The worker was a massive man holding up a hammer and the woman was just as big holding up a sickle and the sheer size of it totally amazed me. I borrowed the book and took it back to my cell and studied every picture inside it and of course read it from cover to cover. I held on to this book and now for a quick confession - I nicked it. When I was released the book came with me and I remember one of the screws questioning me over it. He asked where it came from and I told him that it was brought in for my studies and he just put it down and went through the rest of my stuff. Had he checked I guess I would have been in a bit of bother but this book was such a massive influence the risk was worth it and, for me, it paid off. Back in the classroom I now decided that I wanted to know everything there was to know about the Soviet Union. I read every book there was available and because books on people such as Marx and Lenin were deemed political these were not allowed but there were general histories and I read every one of them intensely. One book I did get my hands on was one on Stalin but I must confess that this really confused me. This man indeed created the world's first superpower with his five year plans and turned Russia from a backward country into an industrial nation. This being the case he was also a bloody mass murderer and killed people if they looked at him wrongly. I then began to get my hands on books about Lenin from another of the instructors who brought them in for me. I don't know much about this teacher but what I do remember was he was one of the CND types who hated nuclear weapons. On reading about Lenin I discovered that the last person who he wanted to take over on his death was Stalin so Lenin became a bit of a hero to me and this remains to this very day.

But why was all this such a turnaround for me? Well the answer is quite simple. Before I had ever seen the book *Portraits of Moscow* I was totally fascinated by Hitler and the Nazis and many a chat was had over the chessboards at association with other inmates. Many of the prisoners from the protestant side were open supporters of the National Front and I must confess that they totally confused me. Here they were preaching about white Britain, white anglo saxon protestants, no black in the Union Jack send the ******* back and all that. They were also going on about how Hitler was right and all that but here's where I got confused. Was Hitler not bombing the shit out of Britain and at war with them? Was Hitler and most of the Nazi high command not Catholic? I was totally lost.

One of these inmates whom I remember being National Front mad was a guy called Lamont from Coleraine and I often think of him today and wonder what became of him. The others I know what happened. One of them was a lad by the Name of William 'Budgie' Allen who got tied up with the UVF and went on to become a supergrass which was a protected informer squealing on quite a few of his mates. Two of the others were Johnny Adair and Sam "Skelly' McCrory and if memory serves me right both were photographed glue sniffing at a National Front march in Belfast shortly after our release.

Sam 'Skelly' McCrory pictured inside the H Blocks

Much has been written about Adair and people can therefore make their own minds up about him. When Johnny Adair mania was going though Belfast about his killing abilities I knew it was untrue as I knew he didn't have the ability to be a terrorist godfather. I knew he was a front and that the killings were in fact being carried out by his friend who lived over in Manor Street and who has since died. Skelly was a different kettle of fish as they say in Belfast. He was intelligent and both of us had many a conversation over a chess game. I know what Skelly became and I also know that it was friends of his who killed my future wife's brother when they walked into his house and gunned him down as he was making his families dinner. Naturally you would automatically assume that I would detest him but if it were not for Skelly then the simple fact of the matter is you would not be reading this today.

A few years later a gang of loyalists jumped me when I got on a wrong bus in Belfast city centre. There was a bomb scare and I got on a bus which I thought was going up to the Antrim Road. The said bomb scare was on the Antrim Road and instead it went along York Street and it was there that the loyalists got on. One of them recognised me as we worked on a YTP scheme together and they all jumped me and proceeded to beat the hell out of me. Some of them were screaming to keep me down and bring me to the village to kill me. Judging by the direction of the bus the 'village' they were talking about was Rathcoole on the outskirts of North Belfast. Skelly was there and when he saw who I was he got them all off me and shouted that he knew me and that I was alright. He picked me up, asked if I was ok, and helped me off the bus. Would they have killed me? Yes of course they would but one thing about that incident baffles me to this day. Why did the bus driver not drive to the nearest police station?

Anyway, getting back to Hydebank, I was reading everything I could get my hands on about the Soviet Union and about communism and talking it over with the other inmates. Most of them hadn't a clue what the hell I was talking about except one. He was called Charlie and was from Derry and my impression of him was that he seemed to know everything there was about politics. He was also fascinated by space exploration and was able to tell me that it was really the Soviet Union who won the space race. This was 1981 and he was able to tell me then (long before the internet) that it was doubtful that the United States had ever went to the moon.

Yuri Gagarin

Laika

Valentina Tereshkova

Belka and Strelka

He explained to me that even if they had that it was the Soviets who put the first satellite into space (Sputnik), the first living creature (Laika) the first living creatures to return (Belka and Strelka) the first man (Yuri Gagarin) and the first woman (Valentina Tereshkova). Charlie told me that on these alone and granting the Americans the moon landing the Soviets had won 5-1. However there were many other firsts ranging from the first moon landing (unmanned) and deep space satellites. Back in the classroom I wanted to learn everything there was to learn about this Space Race and learn I did. This American/Soviet stuff also came in with our instructor who we were placed with for our work placement. If you remember he was into all the nuclear disarmament stuff and he fascinated me about all the Cold War.

He, rightly, told me that there was no winners in a nuclear conflict as the world would be totally destroyed as each superpower, especially Russia, had enough nuclear weapons to destroy the planet ten times over. He also used to preach about how one of the biggest war crimes of the Second World War was the atomic bombing of Hiroshima and Nagasaki but in fairness to the Americans I don't think they really knew what they were dealing with other than one hell of a big bomb.

In our work placements we were doing several different courses with my favourite being painting and decorating. Here I learned all the tricks of the trade such as the difference between paints, brushes and of course how to clean up afterwards. One day I got into a fight with a lad from Divis Flats and I threw a bucket of paint over him so that was my painting a decorating hit on the head as I was thrown of the course and onto the boards for another read of the bible. I don't know what they were more annoyed about - the fact that I threw the paint over him or the fact that I made sure it was gloss! However it was only a one off fight and a few years later he got himself into a situation where he was shot dead by the IRA.

On being released from the boards I was then placed into industrial cleaning where we had to clean all the non wing sections of the building. This was meant to be the bottom of the pit but I absolutely loved it. What our job was was to clean the administration section of the prison, the visiting area as well as all the offices. It was bloody great as were the perks. We had freedom to move throughout the whole prison and when in the visiting area we also had access to the supplies of the

tea shop - what more could you ask for! Our instructor was a man named Ferguson and there are two things I remember about him. The first was his size and if I remember rightly I think he was one of those power weightlifters. The second was he had previously worked with my da and was quite friendly with him. When he asked me about him at the start I denied knowing anybody called Charlie Baker which was understandable given my experience with 'Nixon' previously. However Mr Ferguson persisted and kept going on and on about how his friend Baker was from the New Lodge and that I was from the same area and had the same name so I guess the game was up and I touched lucky. Shortly before this my da came up on a visit and I asked him about Mr Ferguson and my da told me they were good friends and that he was indeed a nice man. A nice man he was and I can state now that he would have done anything for you. There were four of us on the industrial cleaning squad and two of them were from the New Lodge area, Martin Murphy and Sean Collins who was a childhood friend and who was with me at the infamous Waterworks incident mentioned previously.

Part of our duties in this squad were cleaning the offices in the administration block and this gained us access to items such as sugar. In prison sugar is worth its weight in gold as it is one of the forbidden products. A pouch of this gained you half an ounce of snout (Old Holborn tobacco) and sugar cubes - well they were something else. We also had access to coffee and what this got us was beyond belief. I got snout, biscuits and numerous bars of chocolate so much in fact that I never had to use the tuck shop at the end of the week. The tuck shop was where you went on a Friday to spend your whole £2 earned for your work duties. You got your goodies in but, as I said, mine was a bonus as I didn't need it due to my sugar and coffee racket. I also had another racket on the side. When you sent your clothes to the laundry they came back clean but unironed. I was quite good at ironing and I would iron other inmates clothes for packets of biscuits, snout, chocolate and my all time favourite fruit shortcake. To say overall I had quite a scam going would be an understatement. There was another scam which I had going and although it started of as a racket it soon developed into something else completely.

Some of the inmates couldn't read and write and for some reason they came to me for help. They would ask me to read their letters to them and reply to them by writing out what they were saying. For me it was practice but to them it was a lifeline. Sometimes the letters I got were heartbreaking to say the least and to get an idea of what I'm talking about think 'Dear John!' Some of them broke my heart and there was no way I could tell them what the letters really said. What I did was went with the flow and told them the true story the day before their release but I often think of those who stayed behind when my release came around first. In Hydebank I really was everything from a shit scrubber to a communist ideologist, a damned good ironer and, in a round about way, an agony aunt! But what did I do? What did I do to chill out from all this mayhem? The answer is quite simple - pottery! In the education block there was a pottery room next to the library and this was my deep dark cave in which to retreat into. I loved pottery and you take my word for it there is nothing more relaxing - think Demi Moore and Patrick Swayze in Ghost and you'll know what I'm on about. In the pottery room I went on to develop a knack for building Irish cottages and to do this, and get the detail right, I built them brick by brick. This involved making tiny bricks from solid clay and sticking them together with watery clay and in the end what I created was a bloody masterpiece once it was painted and fired. The governor wanted a few as did every other screw

who had obviously forgot their wive's birthday or anniversary. This earned me quite a few brownie points in the "favour owed department" but here's a strange fact to dwell over. Since my release from Hydebank in the early 1980's I have moved house several times and do you know that right up to the time of writing I still have the very first cottage I ever made and that in every house I have ever had, it was always kept in the kitchen - as it is today.

Now before you think I have went all arty there was another reason we went to pottery classes and it had absolutely nothing to do with mixing clay. The instructor always had a radio on. This was the only chance we ever got to hear the radio and because the instructor was young enough it was always on Radio 1 instead of some coffin dodger stuff like Downtown. It was only one afternoon a week but it was one afternoon a week we really looked forward to.

Another weekly event I really looked forward to was visits. It was really hard to get a visit for a Saturday as everyone booked these so the more mid week you went the better. Because dad was working he could only get up every other month and I knew it was a massive burden on my mum so luckily I had two close friends who helped out and visited me every other week. These were my friends Paula Graham and Ann Brown. Paula lived in Edward Street behind St Anne's Cathedral and Ann lived in Victoria Parade, yards away from our flat. These two would have brought up a parcel from my mum which consisted of the usual apples and oranges but the one thing I always looked forward to was the Weekly News which, I think, was a Scottish paper and filled with brilliant human interest stories and titbits. Because Paula and Ann were the same age they were able to tell me all the real news such as who was seeing who and who was caught by their parents doing such and such. They didn't realise it at the time but while these two teenage girls looked on a visit to Hydebank as a great adventure, to me it was a vital lifeline.

Life here continued as it did every bleedn day, the same routine only broken up by my numerous days in solitary confinement. I don't know just exactly how much time I spent in Hydebank as I had lost so much remission but I do remember it being autumn when I was released. I know this because the leaves were falling off the trees and given that all the wings in the Young Offenders Centre were named after trees and that Hydebank was indeed Hydebank Wood I guess I was in the right place to know this sort of stuff. When I was released from the YOC I had to walk down the long driveway through Hydebank Wood and I remember looking back and thinking that I won't ever be back there again.

How wrong I was.

NEWS LETTER

MONDAY, NOVEMBER 25, 1991   ULSTER EDITION   EST. 1737   Price 28p (IR 36p in Eire)

New police units step up hours

STAFF REPORTER

THE RUC is putting every available policeman on the streets in a bid to stop the slaughter by terrorists.

A number of temporary mobile support units have been formed across the Province and are working 12 hours at a time.

Their members, many culled from static duties, are being given a crash course on tackling terrorists.

Others have been drafted from regular duties in police stations across the Province.

The stepping up in man-hours is to provide cover in depleted stations and also to curb an escalation of terrorist activity to trouble-free areas.

The highly trained MSUs in Belfast are still working normal shifts — causing ill feeling among members.

They have been concentrating their efforts in the north of the city where there have been more murders per square mile than any other area of the Province.

Several of the new units are believed to be operating in north and south Belfast.

Others have been formed in provincial towns.

The formation of temporary MSUs was a direct response to the upsurge in murders.

Chief Constable Hugh Annesley and Secretary of State Peter Brooke came under fire to clamp down on killers, particularly in the wake of sectarian killings by loyalist and republican paramilitaries.

Jail bomb blast kills prisoner — two others badly hurt
MURDER IN 'C' WING

By MARK SIMPSON

A BOMB blast in Belfast's Crumlin Road jail last night killed a loyalist remand prisoner and injured eight others while they were having their Sunday dinner.

Robert Skey, 27, died when the explosion ripped through the dining hall in C-wing shortly after 5pm. Two of the injured are in a serious condition in hospital.

North Belfast Ulster Unionist MP Cecil Walker claimed a device had been hidden behind a radiator in the room which had been used half an hour earlier by republicans.

Police and several prison officers were treated for shock and it is understood the damage is extensive, heightening speculation that Semtex explosives, a favourite of the IRA, had been used.

Mr Skey, from Boundary Walk in the Shankill area of Belfast, had been on remand awaiting trial for kidnapping and assaulting a Roman Catholic.

His brother William, 28, was shot dead by the outlawed Ulster Freedom Fighters in the loyalist Taughmonagh area of south Belfast just over a year ago for allegedly being an informer.

Earlier, he had been interrogated by RUC detectives at Castlereagh holding centre.

One of the seriously injured prisoners was described last night as "critical", the other "stable".

The other six injured were treated for minor injuries at the Royal Victoria Hospital. It is understood that at least two of the inmates were taken back to the jail.

The troubled top security prison holds about 480 prisoners.

See Page Four

DEATH SCENE: an ambulance drives out of Crumlin Road Jail following last night's explosion — inset, the dead prisoner, Robert Skey.
Picture: Trevor Dickson

MP lashes Stormont

THE Northern Ireland Office was put in the dock last night over the killing of the loyalist remand prisoner in Crumlin Road prison.

North Belfast MP Cecil Walker, a staunch campaigner for segregation at the flash-point Crumlin Road prison, said the Northern Ireland Office should have known that someone was going to die sooner or later.

The Ulster Unionist MP charged angrily: "I hate to say it, but I predicted that this was going to happen.

"I've been pleading for some form of segregation

CECIL WALKER segregation

between the loyalist and republican prisoners for some time. I have been very deeply concerned at recent events, particularly affecting loyalist prisoners.

"We have had loyalists scalded and even attacked with knives. We need some form of segregation on the landings in that jail. We have had nothing but problems."

Mr Walker said he had been inundated by calls from prisoners' relatives anxious to find out if their loved-ones had been caught up in the blast.

"All of them said they could not believe that their relations were not even safe in a Government prison," said the MP.

DUP deputy leader Peter Robinson said the Government must be held responsible for the death of the loyalist prisoner and the injuries inflicted on eight others.

"While prisoners are incarcerated in Her Majesty's jails they are completely the responsibility of the authorities.

"The Minister with responsibility for prisons, Lord Belstead, should resign and a new prison policy to safeguard the lives of prisoners must immediately be introduced," said Mr Robinson, the East Belfast MP.

See Page 2

THE EIGHTIES!

When inside Hydebank Rab Skey and I were separated by wing moves and my only regret when leaving was that I never got to see him again. Rab got himself involved in the UDA and years later was on remand in the Crumlin Road Prison. The next I ever heard of him was in November 1991 when the IRA planted a bomb behind a radiator in the jail and killed two loyalist prisoners. Rab was one of them. Although I never saw Rab again its amazing the amount of people who I had been in Hydebank with who I met again in different surroundings. My release was in the early 1980's and in those days one of the things we used to do was meet various people from all over Belfast in the city centre. For example we met people from loyalist areas in places such as the City Hall and the College of Art in York Street and some of these people I would first have met in Hydebank.

A group of skinheads pictured at Smithfield. Bugsy McAuley is seated in the centre.

Mods pictured outside Lord Hamills in Wellington Place.
Pictures taken from Images of Belfast *by Robert Johnstone and Bill Kirk*

The College of Art

I had met up with people such as Skelly and Johnny Adair and, as previously mentioned Adair never really impressed me but Skelly and I got on quite well. As I stated Skelly was then big time into the National Front but later became involved with the UDA and in one of their murder squads. In a recent television programme Skelly was shown taking part in a Gay Pride parade in Glasgow and many people were shocked that this terrorist godfather would turn out to be gay. I wasn't as that was something that I picked up on way back then. We would also have met up in the town on Saturdays and this was more to do with music more than anything. Punks and skinheads would have congregated at Cornmarket, Mods round at Lord Hamills close to the City Hall and it was rarely that the two would have met. I was different. I seemed to know everybody and on my way into town I was one of the few who could talk to them all and I would have had no problem walking among the mods to talk to someone I knew on my way round to Cornmarket. Now I'm not 100% about this but I think the mods were the only ones who did

not have anywhere to drink. The rockers and teddy boys would have went to Baileys which was behind the Albert Clock and next door was Paddy Reas which is where all the punks went. Around the corner was DuBarrys which was the pick up joint for prostitutes. The whole area is now totally transformed and McHughs Bar takes up this spot and each time I go into it I always have a laugh into myself when I read inside "McHughs - Established 1711." Don't think so!

Anyway it was the rocker types who seemed to have a particular dislike to the mods and it was from hanging out down here that I got to know quite a few of them and, believe it or not, I'm still quite friendly with a lot of them to this day. Although Paddy Reas was our hang out there was another reason why we were down here and that was because it was this area that most of the subways where. Most are now gone but even when they were here with Belfast being Belfast no one used them. This was perfect for us as it meant that we could go down and do the stuff we were not meant to be doing such as sniffing glue and it was there that up to twenty of us would have headed for that purpose.

Me pictured with Henry 'Hen' Brady in the early 1980's. Sadly Hen was later to take his own life

I'm sure you have gathered that I was a punk at this time and although short lived there were quite a few of the bands that we were into then that I still listen to today even though I'm well into my forties. Needless to say the music of the Sex Pistols is eternal but the others we were into were bands such as UK Subs, Crass, Poison Girls, Discharge and the local ones such as Outcasts and Stiff Little Fingers. The punks also had another place to go and that was in a derelict warehouse called The Anarchy Centre which was up a back lane off Lower North Street and in here we could go, pay an admission fee, and drink and sniff glue while watching a live punk band. To be honest I don't remember any of the bands except one but I think that the glue and drink might have had something to do with that! The one band I do remember was brought over from England and that was Poison Girls and they were absolutely brilliant but looking back this place was really a death trap and to be honest I'm surprised no one was ever killed in it or that a fire ever broke out. Its interesting to note that when we look back at the rave and dance scene where they once broke into old factories and warehouse to have their raves that it was happening here years before. I also look at young people today wearing the t shirts of all these bands and just think - remember it all first time round!

Of course it wasn't all meeting up with prods, sniffing glue and going to dodgy underground concerts there was also money to be earned.

When I left Hydebank I enrolled in a YTP (Youth Training Programme) scheme which was situated in the old Ewarts Mill on the Crumlin Road. We were employed at different things ranging from painting and decorating through to bricklaying but very little of it interested me. One section that did was restoring old tools. Old tools were collected and repaired so that they could be shipped out to Africa. This was the section where I spent most of my time as I felt that I was doing something useful. When I started there I remember my dad asking me what the hell I was doing in there as it was run by the UDA. I had no answer as I was sent here by a government agency but the funny thing is my dad was right. The place was run by Davy Payne who was a leading loyalist and who was later caught with a load of weapons.

In these early days of the 1980's my main interest was music and punk rock to me was the greatest thing ever. Having heard it live there was no going back. There was only one other punk in the place and her name was Sadie Moore who lived in the loyalist Glencairn Estate in West Belfast. Her and I talked a lot about our interest in music and soon after we began to go out together. Not long after that we had our first child together and soon after that we were married. That was the extremely short version as the long version was a bloody nightmare. Now here I was, a Catholic from the Nationalist New Lodge area and she a Protestant from the Loyalist Glencairn area so I don't think I need

Me and Doc Doherty

Me and Hazzel Morgan

Piper Morrison and Me

Hazzel, me and Bouncer O'Neill

Hazzel and Bugsy McAuley

Hen Brady and me

Sadie Moore, Hazzel and me

Titch and Roisin

to explain what the problems were. Our first child, David, was born in 1983 and soon after his birth we both moved in together into a flat directly next door to my mum and dad and to give you an idea of how skint we were our furniture came off a nearby bonfire site. Shortly after that we moved to a flat on the Cavehill Road but only stayed there briefly before moving back to the flats in the New Lodge. This time we moved into a top floor flat in what was then called Alexander House and it was here that we were to settle for quite a few years.

Earlier I mentioned about those with musical interest meeting up in town such as mods, skinheads etc. well

there was another group and to be honest I don't think anyone every really bothered with them - heavy metalers. It was also at this training scheme that I first got talking to heavy metal types and the music they were into. One of them let me borrow one of his records which was called We Sold Our Soul For Rock and Roll by a band called Black Sabbath. That album changed my musical influence forever and that band were to become my gods.

When I finished in this training scheme I began another in the Boucher Road area in a complex which is now the training centre for the Northern Ireland Fire Service. Looking back this place was an excellent training facility where you could have learned everything from electrics right through to welding. I have no idea why but I seemed to have developed something of a knack for the electric welding and funny enough a tool box I made in it is still used by me to this day. This is still in one piece so we're talking quality workmanship never mind your Stanley or Black & Decker's! This place was not for me and one day, when feeling really pissed off, I simply walked out the door and never went back.

I don't know if it is the same today but in those days if you quit work or walked out of a training scheme then you could kiss good-bye to your dole money so for me I had to get on a new scheme and get one fast. The one I did get was taken out of desperation as there was nothing else but it was one that was to totally fascinate me and one which turned out to be one of those major life changing efforts! In those days if you had said to

Clifton Street Graveyard before clean up work began

me anything about gardening I would have automatically told you it was for poofters and girls as there was a lot of flowers involved. How wrong I was.

The next training scheme for me was up to a gardening training complex at the old Nutts Corner airfield. I absolutely loved it and was totally fascinated by growing living things from tiny seeds. This fascination was already in me from my visits to my Uncle Davy's garden all those years ago. After this training I got my very first proper job which was with the Belfast City Council Parks Department.

I was so proud of this and getting a whole £92 per week but fate was to play one hell of an unusual trick and that was to do with my placement - Clifton Street Cemetery. Now this was the place where we drank cider, sniffed glue and pushed the odd headstone over for a laugh. Now if you believe the local New Lodge gossips it was also the place where we dug up bodies and held devil worshipping sessions with up to twenty naked girls - I bloody wish!

My boss was Gerry McKeown who was an extremely well known Belfast character. Over the years me and Gerry developed a love hate relationship in that at one time I threw a pickaxe at him and missed his head by about two inches and yet I cried my eyes out when I heard of his death a few years later.

While working at Clifton Street Cemetery I met many new friends and between us all we were to turn the cemetery from an overgrown dump into the peaceful place it is today, so anything wrong I did there was more than made up for in a Karma sort of way, but I still wish the naked girls bit was true!

The City Council had taken over the cemetery from Clifton House (the old Belfast Poor House) around 1979 and at the time I started they had just received a massive grant from the Belfast Action Team (later BRO) to fix the whole place up. Fix it up we did but the place has never been open to the public even though the Council have sign posts bringing visitors up to it! While working in the cemetery our work hut was actually in the grounds of Clifton House and while down there I got to know some of the staff. One day during a causal chat I was told about the records kept by Clifton House on the cemetery and I asked if I could have a look at them. Guess what - one of those life changing moments occurred again only this time this one was to be major!

RED STAR RISING

Looking at the picture on the back cover it will be noticed that in addition to my musical taste I was also beginning to express an interest in politics and this is given away by the red star I am wearing on my coat. I have absolutely no hesitation in admitting that I am a communist plain and simple. I don't try and break the whole thing down into Marxist, Leninist, Socialist or, for the more extreme, Stalinist. I really do believe that everyone is born equal in that they come out of their mums as bloody crying sprogs!

This being the case I don't believe that people go on to be equal and to give an example and allow you to make up your own mind think of someone who becomes a great doctor and another who becomes an abuser of children. Are they equal!

I am not going to go into a whole political debate in explaining my communist beliefs but for those who will state that it doesn't work as the Soviet Union collapsed then look again. Corruption and greed brought down the Soviet Union not its political system. However, its interesting to note that in recent times when we see the failures of capitalism in that it nearly collapsed then the communist policy of nationalisation is what turned out to save it with the governments of the western world having to buy out the banks (for future readers look up Northern Rock.) Anyway I continued my reading on the politics of the Soviet Union and slowly introduced myself into other similar subjects such as Cuba and Che

Guevara. This all totally blew me away but it was all nothing compared to a single image I was to see on a trip to the Imperial War Museum in London.

My visit to London was as part of an award ceremony for an exhibition I was part of through Artillery Youth Club for a major photographic exhibition on the New Lodge in which we were presented with an award from the Duke of Westminster. We picked up the said reward in a military barracks and while there I decided I would explore London.

I went and saw all the sights as would be expected and one of them was the Imperial War Museum. There they had a massive image on the wall of a young child moments from death with a vulture behind it waiting on the poor child to die so that it could eat it. When I saw that picture I just sat down facing it and stared at it for what must've been hours.

It was that picture that made me realise that things in this world are not right given the fact that there were those who could spend a quarter of a million quid on a handbag and others where a mere £2 could save their sight and that £1 could feed them for a month. It was at the same time that the famous Live Aid stuff was going on and I think I must have been the only person who saw through the propaganda. I remember watching this Bob Geldof inspired event and one of the videos showed a massive plane full of food landing on an air strip in Ethiopia. When the plane was landing it showed, in the

The Barrack area throughout the Troubles was seen as a stronghold of the Official IRA and then the Erps

background, a line of massive Russian/Soviet planes full of aid which were at least twice the size of the one landing. These planes did not even get a single mention.

I knew I wanted to change things not only locally but globally. I got involved in the local Sinn Fein youth but soon after realised it was not for me. I lived in the Barrack area of the New Lodge and that area throughout the Troubles was seen as a stronghold of the Official IRA and then the Erps which was the IRSP and INLA. When I was involved with Sinn Fein youth I was constantly jeered as being a Provie Lick (IRA supporter) and as a result I had to stick with the people I knew so I had to leave Sinn Fein youth.

If you were to ask anyone today what is the New Lodge area they will tell you that it the area bordered by North Queen Street, Duncairn Gardens, Antrim Road and Clifton Street however there are those who state that they are not from the New Lodge and are from The Barrack which is the area roughly between the New Lodge Road and Clifton Street and is based on the site of the old Victoria Military Barracks. You have no idea of the arguments there have been over the years over this but I have found a settlement which keeps both sides happy and that is I simply state that I am from the Barrack area of the New Lodge!

I have already stated that we moved into Churchill House in the late 1960's when I was just four years of age. My first memories of growing up here was the view from the roof of the flats. My dad was the care-taker and he took me up there when he had to clean the engine room and to me the view was just breathtaking (it still is!) At the front of the flats I remember looking down on the remaining section of Victoria Barracks which was being demolished at the time to clear the way for the construction of Carlisle Estate. This was an adventure playground for us and, to be quite honest, I'm surprised none of us ever got killed considering some of the things we got up to in it. In a short time the last of Victoria Barracks was gone and work began on the estate. One thing that I can remember about this was the extremely short time in which Carlisle Estate was erected. One minute they were laying the foundations and when you came back a few days later the house was there.

The flats throughout the 1970's were quite a strong community and while I liked most of those who lived there I must confess that there were also those whom I detested but thankfully these were only a few. Now I admit that in growing up I was no angel but there was one person in particular who blamed me on absolutely everything that happened. On one occasion she went to the local 'police force' and brought them to our flat. Once there she stated that she had saw me breaking the two lifts the night before with a hammer and that everyone had to walk up and down the stairs. Understandably everybody in the whole block were fuming at this but imagine the surprise on that woman's face when my mum turned to her and factually told her that I had been in hospital the past five weeks. Needless to say she stormed out and right up until the day she died there was never even a 'sorry for my mistake.'

Next to Churchill Flats was the hangout of the famous (or is it infamous) Barrack Bonfire Gang and looking back with a sensible head on I really am surprised that no one was ever killed during their exploits. In the overall New Lodge area there were quite a few bonfire gangs during the summer months and these were The Barrack, The Piggy, Carlisle, Sheridan, Bruslee and Glenrosa but the two with the most hatred for each other were The Barrack and Sheridan as the others didn't really count. The rivalry between these two was so intense that all sorts of dirty tricks were entertained including the burning of each others wood in order to have the biggest bonfire. Now I know I'm being biased here when I say that The Barrack had the biggest but there are old Sheridan members who dismiss photography (right) and state that their 'bonie' was always the biggest - a debate which still goes on. As many older people will remember the original bonfires on the Catholic side were lit on the 15th of August but after internment they were lit on the 9th, the first being on the 9th of August, 1972 as part of a protest campaign. At that time the bonfires were quite small compared to what they developed into which was after the 'competition element' came in. Collecting wood began around the end of June and for the kids of the estate this work was carried out day in, day out, and then there was the graveyard shift. They guarded the wood through the night usually by sneaking out of the house through their bedroom window. The Barrack was weak in this department as most of the gang lived in the flats and climbing out the window was a wee bit out of the question!

For collecting purposes our travels took us far and wide and we gathered wood and tyres from the Docks, Sailortown and as far away as the Markets. Old houses were stripped and I remember one of the biggest Barrack bonfires occurred after Glenravel Street RUC Barracks was stripped of all its combustible material (after the lead and copper was taken of course!)

Then there was the raids which, for those not in the know, was the stealing of each others wood and tyres. In this aspect I must admit that The Barrack were the most prolific and most evil because what they could not carry off they burned. I can remember a delegation being sent over to the Bruslee gang on the New Lodge Road to discuss a joint raid on the Piggy which was in North Queen Street. The Barrack were to go down from their area at 3.00pm and Bruslee were to do the same. Come the arranged time a placed scout had reported that Bruslee had all gone down the New Lodge Road after which The Barrack went across and took every single one of Bruslee's tyres. There was not a lot they could do about it because The Barrack

The Sheridan bonfire in 1986

The Barrack one in the same year

had strength in numbers but there is no doubt that it was a devious move which I know Bruslee saw the funny side off later. In fact most of their bonfire gang merged with The Barrack as did Carlisle and The Piggy so that in the end there was only two gangs left with the rivals being Sheridan.

The Barrack also suffered as a result of raids with most of the attacks merging from the Unity Flats gang. This was one bonfire gang which we found quite difficult to break as we found out over the years that over there people never seem to sleep as 5am raiding parties were always detected. But an arrangement was reached and each agreed to leave each other alone. One of The Barrack's strong points in defence was the fact that it was situated next to the tower block of Churchill which meant that attacks on raiders could be made from the roof. During these bricks were thrown and today I must admit that I am glad that we missed our targets as a brick from this height would have undoubtedly killed whoever it struck.

These raids were never confined to rival gangs within the area as many a raid was done by The Barrack on bonfires in the Bone, Markets and, believe it or not, Loyalist areas. One such raid I remember was on the Loyalist bonfire on the Shore Road facing the Grove Baths when a 5am raid resulted in a massive amount of tyres being taken but looking back on this now the hairs on the back of my neck stand - could you imagine if we had been caught!

In the days before the bonfire a last minute push was made to get as much material as possible if it was looking as if Sheridan were getting the upper hand but other raids included excursions into Loyalist areas again in order to obtain flags for said bonfire. For The Barrack gang the easy pickings were Clifton Street Orange Hall and the Shankill Estate. What occurred here was a few on the graveyard shift would enter the area and quietly remove flags flying outside the houses. Another competition was to see which gang could get the most flags but, once again looking back, this was nothing more than out and out madness as the consequences of being caught are not even worth thinking about.

Come the 8th of August the bonfire now resembled a construction site. It was then that the men came out and piled up the tons of wood with the kids acting as an army of ants in bringing the wood up to them. Once erected everyone then went and got ready for the night including a good bath and the compulsory carry out. At the Barrack site the one thing that always amazed us was the number from the Shankill Estate who came to watch. They gathered on the hill at the back of the Orange Hall with their carry outs and that was them getting to watch another bonfire, have a drink and do no work towards it whatsoever - and who can blame them. After all they gave us a bonfire to watch on the 11th of July and an excuse to get a carry out.

This brings me to a more sinister side of bonfire time. There was one occasion on said 11th night when a guy in a Glasgow Rangers shirt approached the night shift of the Barrack gang and, in a broad Scottish accent which nobody could understand, asked "what time are yous lighting your fire at?" Everyone was in total disbelief at what was going on before their eyes when he stated that "the boys over there sent me down to ask what time you're lighting your fire at." A few of the more sensible members of the gang then got the guy, took him down to North Queen Street Peeler Barrack and told them what happened. The Peelers in turn got him into a Landrover and wanted him to point out who sent him down. Whatever happened to him or if they got those involved we never found out but what I still find hard to believe is the fate that those who sent him thought they were sending him to and I'm glad that the more sectarian elements of the gang were in bed when

The Barrack gang were that mad they even raided loyalist bonfires

this occurred as my heart really went out to him and his total misunderstanding of what he was doing.

Today I'm glad that these bonfires no longer exist as I now realise the nuisance they must have been to the local community but in their defence I must admit that they were perfect for keeping kids occupied throughout the Summer because I remember when they were over the few weeks we had to wait to get back to school were hell as we were so bored.

There are still bonfires in Loyalist areas in July and I really think that that community really need to wise up to the destruction and cost of these. To be honest I don't mind if they burn wood but when you see all the tyres going up in smoke then we really need to think of the environment on this one, especially when we see bonfires made of nothing but tyres. Now I know no one on the Loyalist side is really going to listen to me on this one but I would point out one thing that was pointed out to me during a Barrack bonfire when I had my first child on my shoulders watching the huge blaze. "With all these tyres burning," he said, "imagine what that child is breathing in."

Developments saw the end of bonfires in the New Lodge area. Star of the Sea School and the Ashton Centre took Sheridan's spot and the Westlink, houses and a park saw the end of the Barrack's sacred place but to this day the arguments between The Barrack and Sheridan continue as to who had the biggest "bonie."

(Incidentally it was The Barrack!)

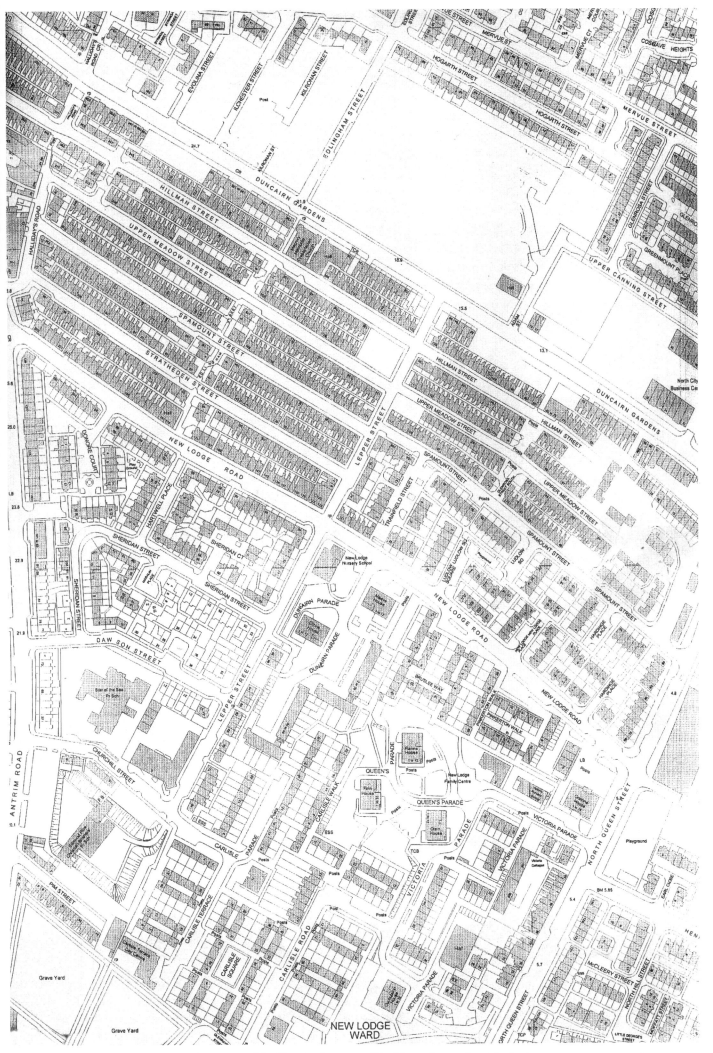

A modern map of the New Lodge area. The Barrack area is at the bottom

THE ERPS

The December 1969 split within the IRA left the Provisional's as a growing force, and as the conflict reached severe proportions in 1972, the Provisional's arose as the dominant force, carrying the mantle of the IRA following the Official's ceasefire the same year. This left those remaining within the Officials feeling the need for some political rethinking, and a sense of direction in strategy. For some, there was only one course open, a return to the militant stance. They felt the leadership had failed them, and thus the Irish Republican Socialist Party came into being in December 1974. They provided an outlet for those 'Officials' who wished to return to armed struggle. The climax of this internal split came in April 1975 when it overflowed into a feud resulting in the death of the Official's officer commanding, Billy McMillen.

The IRSP's military wing, the Irish National Liberation Army (INLA) had sprung on to the political landscape. Their numbers were never to reach a scale to match the IRA, but they would leave their mark on the history of the Irish conflict.

They drew their recruits mainly from the lower Falls, the Markets, Short Strand, the Barrack and South Derry. Members engaged in sniping and bombings and their presence was consumed into the daily on-going 'Ulster

Conflict', until one day in March 1979, when a bomb explosion in the heart of London shook the British establishment. Airey Neave, the Conservative spokesman on the North was killed in a bobby trap explosion within the House of Commons carpark. He was a a a war hero and personal friend of the Margaret Thatcher, who became Prime Minister two months later.

Despite having experienced IRA bombings in the past, Airey Neave's death struck home. The killing was claimed by the INLA for what they said was his rapid militarist calls for more repression against the Irish people. (This was at a time before the IRA attacks at the Brighton Hotel where the Conservative Government were holding a conference and the mortar attack on 10 Downing Street during a War cabinet meeting) and such an attack within the compound of the British House of Commons, sent shock waves through the British Government.

The same year the IRA killed Lord Mountbatten, the Queen's uncle. Two years later, during the Hunger Strikes, Thatcher would not forget both killings and they obviously had a strong bearing on her opposition to restoring political status.

In 1982, the INLA were responsible for 30 deaths 17 of whom died in an explosion at the Droppin Well in Ballykelly, Co. Derry on the 6th of December. The bar was used by off duty British troops from the nearby Shackleton Barrack, which dominates the garrison village.

They also carried out several attacks on Loyalist paramilitary figures and Unionist politicians. Their first victim was Loyalist John McKeague, said to have been killed by members of a small INLA unit operating from the Short Strand. These attacks would continue until their ceasefire in August 1998 with one of their last victims being the notorious Loyalist killer Billy Wright who they shot dead inside the H-Blocks.

But the organisation was plagued by internal feuding, often sparked by personality problems or policy direction. These disputes resulted in some of the main figures within the organisation dying at the hands of former comrades, while during the 1981 hunger strike, three of the ten came from the INLA whose prisoners numbered some 28, against the IRA's 380.

When they called their ceasefire in August 1998, they apologised for any innocent deaths they may have caused, but refused to apologise for their war against the "British and their Loyalists associates."

One name that stands out in the INLA's history is that of Ronnie Bunting, one of the organisations founding members.

His background was not in the mould of the normal INLA member. He arose from a middle class Protestant background, his father being ex-British Army and hard line Unionist stalwart Major Bunting.

Ronnie graduated from Queen's University to become a school teacher, but at the same time he grew into socialism and became involved in the Civil Rights Movement in 1968.

When the conflict broke out in 1969, his experience of witnessing social injustice and sectarian pogroms, caused him to join the IRA.

He was interned between November 1971 and April 1972 and had been active around the lower Falls area. When his political thinking moved him towards the IRSP, he was shot and wounded by the Official's in March 1975 after the split. But when the end came on the night of 15th October 1980, no shade of Republicanism were responsible for his death, as an assassination squad broke into his home in the heart of Andersonstown, and with ruthless military precision shot and killed Ronnie Bunting and his close associate Noel Lyttle, a member of the IRSP National H-Block Committee. Lyttle had just been released from the

Castlereagh Interrogation Centre and was staying with the Bunting's. It was clear those who carried out the killings knew they were in a position to remove two of the IRSP's leading figures in one attack.

At the inquest Bunting's father said of his son:- *He was a virtuous and high minded man who had a keen sense of social justice and fought oppression and injustice where ever he saw it.*

Ironic words from a man who once walked side by side with Ian Paisley, and died three years later having turned his back on politics.

ESCAPES AND MURDER ATTEMPTS

At this stage I was living in the middle of the Barrack at no 12 Alexander House where I had settled with Sadie after we had our first child David. Soon after we were married and soon after that came our second child, Charlene, who was born in April 1987. I was still working away with the Parks Department and it was also around this time when my political interests came closer to home.

Within the New Lodge area I was witnessing people I knew quite well being gunned down by loyalists including a friend of mine, Billy Kane, who was shot in his mothers house as he lay sleeping. Loyalists also killed another guy I knew, Gary Campbell, as his two year old child watched. The British Army were also doing their bit and one such shooting was that of Peter McBride, whom I knew very well, who was shot dead by trigger happy soldiers as he fled being harassed by their armed patrol. These are just an example – there were many, many more.

Billy Kane   *Gary Campbell*   *Peter McBride*

Because I was from the Barrack, the organisation I was to become involved with was the Erps. I did not become full time member but instead stayed on the fringes. Needless to say it was not long before I came to the attention of the RUC. Like my earlier convictions I cannot go into detail on anything as I can't remember what I got caught doing and what I got away with so you'll have to forgive me if I become a bit vague! One thing I can state for a fact is that I never killed anyone not because of any conscious decision but because my talents were used else where.

One place I got quite used to was Castlereagh Interrogation Centre which was notorious for the torture tactics used by the RUC. However this being the case I can honestly state that I never had a finger laid on me there once even though I must have been dragged in dozens of times. It was also here that informers were recruited and I have heard the stories of suitcases of money being offered – all I was ever bloody offered was a tenner a week! When taken to Castlereagh you sat and kept your mouth shut and that was it. I remember a friend and I being taken there and he took the sit down and shut up policy one step further. If they wanted to interview him they had to carry him to the interrogation room and likewise when

Castlereagh Interrogation Centre

he was to go back to his cell. He never ate, drank water – absolutely nothing. Both of us were released a few days later and to be honest I think they were glad to see the back of him.

North Queen Street Barracks was a different case altogether. This was situated in the Barrack area next to the Westlink and to say that I got beat in here would be an understatement. I ended up getting the upper hand as I escaped from this place not once but twice! The first time I was arrested at around 6am, taken to North Queen Street and told to sit at reception. When the cops went through to the area behind their reception I don't think that they realised that they had left me sitting alone so I simply stood up and walked out the front door. I still had the security sanger to get through which was the entrance and exit in a massive security fence which surrounded the building. When I got there one of the peelers commented about "that being a quick visit." I replied that it was my brother Joe they had been looking for and just walked on out. Once outside I calmly crossed the road over to the Lancaster Street area and then ran like hell. Needless to say I was now 'on the run' and the peelers were looking everywhere for me. But where do you think I was hiding out? Across the border? South Armagh? America perhaps! I was staying in a friends house directly facing my mum's and it took the cops three months to catch me and even that was by accident. I was taken back to North Queen Street Barracks and given a quick beating in the landrover on the way.

North Queen Street R.U.C. Barracks with our flats in the background

Once inside I was violently thrown about and one peeler pushed right up into my face and snarled "There'll be no fucking walking out the door for you, you fenian fucking bastard." He was right as this time I went over the wall.

When they took me in they held me in behind the secure doors to be processed and the peeler they left in charge of me must have weighed at least 25 stone which is why I guess he was behind the desk. Spotting this I took a bolt for the secure exit which is where they board the landrovers under cover so that snipers can not open up on them. Once out the door I climbed up one of the supports which held the anti rocket mesh on top of the walls and made my escape across the Westlink. It then took them another few months to catch up with me. Once they did they took no chances and threw me straight into a cell and soon after took me to Castlereagh. Here I was questioned for five days and then released so my great escapes had been for nothing but well worth

it as I'm sure it must've really annoyed them not once but twice and in a row!

In terms of my great escapes there was one thing the cops had failed to grasp. North Queen Street was the replacement for the nearby Glenravel Street Barracks and when it was getting built in the early 1970's I literally lived next door as there was no Westlink then. Everyday I was over watching the workmen and at night we sometimes stayed with the watchman if we were allowed. Because of this I knew North Queen Street Barracks like the back of my hand!

I had lost my job at this stage as being in the one place for most of the day was not only risky in terms of searching peelers but also for loyalists. The UVF had made two attempts with the first at the cemetery but they should've consulted a bit more with their source of intelligence as I had left some months before. The second time really was a close call. I was walking up Churchill Street when a car suddenly pulled up in front of me. As soon as it did I instantly recognised the bloke in the back seat and in a split second I jumped over the fence of Pim Street School. The guy in the passenger side pulled out a revolver but I knew to run in a zig zag and he never fired. I then jumped over a small wooden fence, down a steep embankment and away I went. Moments later I felt a warm sensation on my foot. I had badly cut it jumping over the fence but never felt a thing until I was well away – adrenaline is a wonderful thing!

It was not long before the peelers caught up with me, when I was caught inside the British RAF Memorial Club. The cops were delighted and I got done for breaking in but if they had searched the next door derlict a tiny bit more they would have found out what I was really up to. When they surrounded the building I was able to get into a derlict house next door and cover my tracks and hide quite a few items underneath the floorboards. At court I was sentenced to a year back in Hydebank but if I stayed out of trouble then I would be out in six months so that was my plan.

Just like the first time I decided that I would split my day with education and work training and I was shocked to discover that this time I could do education in whatever morning or afternoon suited me. This I did and the first three I picked were the three periods of PE and as a result I never had to go anywhere near the gym and not one person noticed. In the Education Block I decided to concentrate on my reading and writing again and the teacher I had this time around was Mrs Paton. She was absolutely brilliant and a lot of my writings today are down to her. In addition to the reading and writing she taught me grammar. I also continued reading all the material on the Soviet Union but as well as this I began to read books on British history. Back in my wing one of the screws saw these books in my cell and asked me was I into all this stuff. I told him that I liked reading about history and the British books were just the ones I was going through at the moment. He told me of his fascination with the British army and about being in the TA many years ago and being based in Victoria Barracks. He was totally amazed when I was able to tell him the basic history of the barrack and that I lived on its former site. As a result he began to bring me in books on different regiments of the British army and I read every single one. At the back of one of them I saw listed a book which was all about the Irish regiments of the British army and one time I asked him if he could get it. "What the f*** do you think I am a f****** library service" was his instant reply. I stated that I was just asking and walked on to go about doing what I was doing. The following morning the book mysteriously appeared in my cell when I was at education.

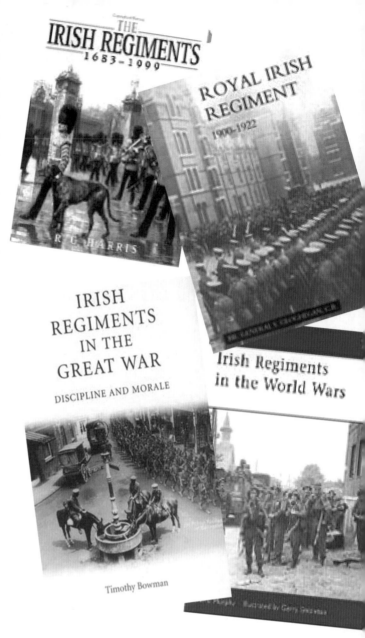

Timothy Bowman

My work placement was over in the main workshops where we were doing painting. Different things were brought in belonging to different charities and we would have fixed them up and painted them. The one I was working on was a bloody yacht and all I remember about this task was it needed about two bloody hundred coats of varnish!

I did not stay in the workshops long before I landed a nice cozy orderly job. The orderlies stayed behind in the wing when all the other prisoners were out and had everything ready for breakfast, dinner and supper. Food was delivered up from the kitchens in large heated trolleys and we had to serve it for the wing kitchen. The only downfall about doing this was you had to get up before all the other prisoners but everything else was a bonus. You got the biggest portions so you never went hungry. You kept the wing hard man well fed so you never got beat up and in the afternoons you could go to your cell and have a nap. To get the orderly job was extremely hard and I later discovered that it was the military loving screw who got me the placement. Things this time around in Hydebank were uneventful and in a few months time I was out again.

THE CRUM

I was not to be out long when a Royal Mail van was hijacked by a number of men, mysteriously burst into flames across the road and I just happened to be in the immediate vicinity. This time I was remanded to the Belfast Prison on the Crumlin Road and all I remember about this place is the fact that it was a dirty hole. I was processed through the reception area and then taken to what was called the basement. This was the bottom floor of D Wing and you stayed here until a cell was ready for you in one of the wings. I was placed in A Wing at A2, Cell 20 and had a lovely view of the top section of the Crumlin Road Courthouse. Before I was moved up I was asked what I was – Republican, Loyalist or ODC (ordinary decent criminal). The purpose of this was to ascertain where you went. My reply was republican and so I was placed with the republican prisoners in the jail.

The reception area of Crumlin Road Jail

There are those who think that loyalists had one wing and republicans another and that they were kept well apart. Nothing could have been further from the truth. One cell would have been Republican and the next Loyalist and so on. Prisoners arranged their own segregation in that one day Republicans would have went out while Loyalists stayed in their cells and the following day vice versa. As soon as I went on to the wing I was questioned by the IRA wing commander on what I was in for but I informed him I was associated with the IRSP and so the INLA commander questioned me. The purpose of this was to ensure I was in for a political offence and to make sure there were no criminal elements on the wings. Once 'my approval' came through I was then taught the drill for parade and taught basic Irish for commands during lock up. I always thought this useless because it was well known than many of the screws and loyalists had learned Irish. A few days after my arrival I was visited by my dad and he had warned me about the jokes they played on prisoners and what to watch out for. The two that I remember were the Sinn Fein doctor and Sinn Fein

priest (a prisoner with his shirt on backwards). The 'doctor' was to examine you to record any injuries picked up during your interrogation in Castlereagh. To do so he took you to a cubicle and asked you to strip. Once you did this he grabbed your clothes and threw them up onto the barbed wire outside leaving you standing naked like a right wally! The 'priest' took you to the same cubicle to hear your confession and once told he went out and shouted to everyone what you had just told him. There were many other pranks and one time one of the IRA men handed a new prisoner an orange with a bit of wire hanging out of it. He was informed that there was going to be a break out and that inside the orange was a grenade and when he got a certain signal he was to pull out the wire and throw the 'grenade' at the sentry post on top of the wall. This was done on lots of new prisoners and it really was a sight to be seen especially when the prisoner ran for cover waiting for the orange to explode. I remember thinking that they'll never get me with anything as stupid as that but as the old saying goes never say never. One day in the canteen I was approached by one of the IRA prisoners and told that next week there was going to be a break out of IRA prisoners and because I was

Some of the new prisoners had to throw a 'grenade' at the sentry post on top of the wall.

The Belfast Prison on the Crumlin Road which was better known as 'The Crum'

not an IRA member I could not be in on it but that my help was needed. I was then told to keep my mouth shut and wait for further instructions. The guy who approached me was a pretty serious bloke and never bothered with all this messing around so I took him very seriously. The following week I was approached by another IRA man out in the yard and told what I was to do.

When the prisoners went out into the exercise yard you could sit around, play football or go for a walk around the yard in a constant circle. When the prisoners were

When the prisoners were out in the yard a screw stood at this door and kept watch.

out a screw stood at the door and kept watch. I was informed that I was to distract him and that me and another prisoner were to walk around the yard three times and when we got round to the screw we were to start fighting. This we did and when we were both on the ground punching the head of each other I caught a glimpse of the screw and noticed that he was laughing his head off. We both then stopped and noticed that the whole yard was in laughter at our expense. I got up and shouted to the IRA group that they were nothing but a bunch of provie bastards and then went and huffed for the rest of the day. A few days later the exact same joke was played on another new prisoner only this time he was to pretend to take an epileptic fit and it was only then that I saw how funny the whole episode was and stopped huffing. The serious IRA prisoner who first informed me of the planned breakout was Ruby Davidson who was shot dead by loyalists soon after his release.

Believe me these pranks and jokes had an impact on future decisions. For example I remember at one time an order was given out that everyone was to wreck their cell and this included the Loyalist prisoners. This was part of the demand for segregation and at a certain time a command was shouted in Irish and the next thing I heard all this crashing and smashing. A few minutes

Yours truly pictured at my cell A2 Cell 20

the Markets area of Belfast. The one thing I remember about him was just how intelligent he was and during our lock ups he would often tell me of revolutions in other countries and how successful they were and that the same could be carried out in Ireland. There was only one problem and I never had the nerve to say it to him. Most of the countries he was talking about were totally unheard of to me!

Ta was held due to the evidence given by the supergrass Harry Kirkpatrick and had been here for quite some time. On one occasion Ta and a few other INLA prisoners went on hunger strike protesting at the fact that they were being held under a new form of internment. As I previously mentioned republicans were out one day and locked up the next and during lock up there was no way I could eat in front of him. He told me that there was no problem and for me to eat away but I just couldn't. On the days out I would stuff my face with my parcel goodies and at dinner time I must've set several world records. When it was the turn of the Loyalists to be out the Republicans would go to the canteen and get their food on a tray to go back to their cells and eat it. I would have had mine eaten before I left the canteen never mind by the time I got back to my cell. This was only to last a few days as Ta was moved and I never saw him again.*

later one of the Loyalist leaders shouted out from his cell 'now boys' and all the Loyalists smashed up their cells. I remember sitting in my cell thinking to myself 'yeah right – you'll not catch me out again.' I thought the whole thing was a joke and therefore one cell in the whole block was not smashed up. I had convinced my cell mate that the whole thing was a joke and a few days later we got the heads chewed off us for not taking part. The INLA commander grabbed me to one side and asked me why I had not obeyed the order to wreck the cell. "Wreck the cell" I exclaimed, "I thought you said tidy your cell!" He took one look of disbelief at me and called me a yellow bastard and then stormed off. There was no denial. My cell mate, who was an IRA prisoner, was pulled before his OC and he was told to get off the wing but looking back this was totally unfair as it was me that convinced him that it was all a prank on us. I have no idea why I was not thrown off the wing but at a guess I would think it was down to the fact there there was very few Erp prisoners as it was.

I was not complaining because I now had the cell to myself but this was to change. A lot of the prisoners here were on remand as a result of the supergrass trials and had been here for quite some time. A few days later one of the INLA prisoners was placed in my cell. His named was Thomas 'Ta' Power and he was from

---

*From Wikipedia, the free encyclopedia
Thomas 'Ta' Power was an Irish Republican Socialist who was a leading member of the Irish Republican Socialist Party (IRSP) and Irish National Liberation Army (INLA).
According to the Irish Republican Socialist Movement (IRSM) biography page on Power, he was "from Friendly Street in the Markets area of south Belfast, he had been in the OIRA but joined the INLA in 1975 while a prisoner in Long Kesh."
At age 33, he was shot killed in County Louth alongside Irish National Liberation Army (INLA) leader John O'Reilly by the Irish People's Liberation Organisation which was largely composed of former INLA members as he arrived to negotiate a truce.
Ta Power was a Marxist theorist and historian within the IRSM, who advocated dramatic changes in its strategy and structure. This is the current policy blueprint for the IRSM. These ideas can be read in the 'Ta Power Document' and include the principles of 'collective leadership', 'politics in command' and other concepts Power believed would steer the IRSM away from a military-led strategy. Power's vision was that INLA would become the cutting edge of a new, genuinely all-Ireland, revitalised, revolutionary socialist party and play a secondary supporting role to the IRSM. These ideas were adopted by the INLA just before Power's death and were finally implemented within the movement as a whole under the direction of Gino Gallagher.
Holland and McDonald note in their book on the INLA that "Subordinating military struggle to carefully thought-out political strategy had been Ta Power's dream for a long time. In the 1980s Sinn Fein and the IRA made that a reality with their ballot box come armalite policy. The Provos learnt well from the lessons and mistakes of the IRSP/INLA."

SERVING THE COMMUNITY

It was something that Ta Power had once told me that really made me think. I can't remember the exact words but it was along the lines of the fact that if everyone did a little bit to help working class communities then think what those little bits would add up to! He was right and I believe that the biggest enemy of the working class is the working class themselves because if people stuck together instead of bitching about each other then massive progress could be made to help each other out. I will give an example which I learned in future years. I have no idea the amount of times I have heard "they should do this" and "they should do that." You have no idea the arguments I have got into when I asked who these "they" were.

I got myself involved in community work in the Barrack area of the New Lodge for two reasons. The first was out of a sense of duty because I had been a pain for the local community for a few years and felt it was time to put something back and make up for my mistakes. The second was because I had listened to Ta Power and his 'people doing little bits' lecture which, when you think of it, makes a lot of sense. To jump years ahead and give you an idea of the working class being their worst enemy I will use myself as an example. There are those within my community who get their British Government DLA money and sit in bars and preach about Joe Baker doing this and Joe Baker doing that. Yes, I was a bad boy when I was a teenager and so what, but what about the 25 years voluntary community work?

There are many who think that I get paid a fortune for my work through the Ashton Centre but what would you think if I told you that everything I do for the Ashton Centre and everything I did and do for the New Lodge community for the past twenty five years was totally voluntary? I make my living through my writing and I can assure you I earn every penny I make. To do this I self educated myself, so before you condemn me ask yourself what you are doing for your community and ask yourself if my 25 years of voluntary commitment overcomes a few years of madness when I was a teenager!

My community work began in the Recy when myself and friends attended meetings about anti social activity, we wanted to be there for the bits that we were being blamed for. We showed up and proved that we were nothing more than victims of local gossip. At the same time there was some sort of EEC thing going on where all the material gathered at the infamous EEC food mountains was being given out completely free of charge to those who needed it. I had two problems with this. The first was the sickening realisation that farmers were being paid more not to produce stuff and therefore being kept on EEC subsidies and the second being the food stuff being given out to those who allegedy need it.

To me the people more in need of this EEC surplus food was the starving people of Africa but instead it was given out to the 'starving' people of Belfast.

These thoughts are only later ones and at the time we thought we were doing good for our community. We gathered together and decided that we would help everyone in the area by giving out these EEC freebies and proving that we were not the scum we were made out to be. Over the next few months we gave out boxes of butter, meat and cheese and if memory serves me right the people who objected were the local shop keepers. In a perfect world I could understand where they were coming from, but some of the same shop keepers were coming to some of the delivery people and offering money for the goods that were being delivered free of charge to the local people.

I can honestly state that all of our delivery people told them to clear off but I am aware of quite a few others within the area who didn't and accepted a few quid for what was a massive help to the old people of the area.

If I were asked to name just one person who got me into community work then that person would have to be Moya Hinds. Moya was the community worker based in the Recy and many an argument was had with her about different issues in the area and one day she just turned to me and asked me what I was doing about it? The answer was nothing and I believe that it was from that moment onwards that I decided to be one of those people to make small changes.

But there were indeed other people involved in the Recy who were very instrumental in directing me into the person I am today and names such as Monina O'Prey, Michael Connor and Jimmy Johnston are just three that instantly spring to mind. Jimmy was in charge of the ACE (Action for Community Employment) scheme which ran out of the Recy and it was he who got me started on this. ACE were responsible for painting and decorating old peoples houses and doing their gardens. Because of my gardening know-how I was placed with that squad. That was something that I really enjoyed and over the years I made some very good friends doing it. This scheme was later taken over by Gerry Beattie and through Gerry I got another few years working on this scheme. There are those who criticise the ACE scheme and stopped it but to be honest I think it was a very good programme and something which the government really need to look at again.

L-R. Joe Baker, Kaye Makin, Stick O'Neill, Frankie Donnelly, Kido Friel, Hughie McAuley, Stevie O'Neill, Sean O'Neill and Bouncer O'Neill pictured outside the Recy

It was also through this scheme in the Recy that we were able to pull off some of our pranks on people and some of these remain classics to this day. Now we all know the silly ones like sending someone to a shop to ask for a long weight (long wait!) and to a decorating shop for a bucket of tartan paint but ours were always that little bit better.

It was in the Recy that the New Lodge Festival Committee were based and one of the events organised by them was the fireworks display at Halloween. We would've got a new start and send them to the nearby North Queen Street Barracks with a letter for the desk sergeant which he was told was a fireworks licence which need signing. Once they asked for the desk sergeant and handed it over it was totally unknown to him/her what it really said but to give you an idea it usually went something like this:-

My name is (person with letter) and I would like to confess to the following .... What it really was was a typed confession for every crime that was in the news that week!

ANYTHING FOR A LAUGH!

It's amazing how some things that we do today we have been doing for years without even realising it. For example as a youngster I can remember going into the town every single Saturday with my friends and believe it our not this is something which we still do to this very day. In recent years there were four of us but sadly a few years ago one of our number, Sean McKee, died aged just thirty six. But the tradition still continues. Our routine is generally the same in that we go down to see what is going on and to be honest it is very rarely we actually buy anything!

Our town danders had four die hard members but in recent years one of our number, Sean McKee (seen behind me to the right), died.

This is the man who we went down to see and looking back I wonder if he ever knew his biggest fan base were a bunch of Taigs from the New Lodge! Photograph Bill Kirk

As I said this has been going on now for years and goes right back to the time of my Heavy Metal days when similar people from all over Belfast met at Cornmarket. Once there we would listen to the bible bashers with their loud hailers and the more they burned people in hell then the more we listened. There was one such 'basher' and his speech was the same every week and I have heard it so many times that I can still hear him preach it in my head. It went like this:- "My friends - you are all going to burn in hell. Those Hindus - they're going to hell. The Jews - they're going to hell. Mormons - they're going to hell." He would then go through quite a few different religions before coming to the good bit when he stated:- Protestants, Church of Ireland and Methodists find the Lord Jesus Christ or go to hell. Those who worship false Gods - you're going to hell and as for the Roman Catholics - they're DEFINITELY, DEFINITELY going to hell!" It was at this point that we cheered and clapped but looking back I have often wondered if the said gentleman ever found out that his captive audience was a bunch of Taigs from the New Lodge! I really doubt it but if it kept him happy in his final days then I suppose it was a good thing!

For those visiting the city centre today it seems like an age away from when to enter it you had to be searched before being allowed to proceed. This was carried out at barricades which surrounded the city centre and you lined up to be searched. The said searchers frisked every part of the body and after a while a friend of mine developed this brilliant idea which we looked forward to every week - in fact we paid for it! What happened was that the searchers frisked him and when they came to the bulky item in his coat pocket they asked him what it was. It was then that he stated that he did not know as a man had put something in his pocket and asked him to carry it through and because the job was so boring the searcher thought he had got a result. Now five minutes previously we were round in Gresham Street at one of the pet stores buying a rat so I think you can work out the rest for yourself!

Now I know what you're thinking and that is that there is no way we could have kept this going week in and week out without word getting around the security people and yes - you're right. But once inside the city centre you had to enter the big stores and what did they have at every entrance? Correct - searchers! And because there were so many and they changed nearly every week then they kept this wicked activity of our going a very long time. Looking back I have no idea how many rats we purchased for this activity as on each occasion they were allowed to run free but I can tell you it was without doubt the best scheme we had ever thought of. It's hard to believe that it got better because once we had female members of our Saturday gang who were not afraid of the said rodents then that made the response ten times better. They had to be searched by female searchers and try and imagine the response when they put their hands into the pockets and discovered a live rat at their finger tips - priceless memories!

During the Troubles people going into the city centre had to be searched. This led to some brilliant opportunities for us!

But this now brings me on to the subject of practical jokes a few of which were mentioned in the previous chapter and over the years I must admit that I have been behind quite a few of them. However the best one ever occurred when I was in St Patrick's Training School on the Glen Road. Now we had to go to Mass twice a week, every Wednesday and Sunday. The reason for the Wednesday service was due to the boys who got out at the weekend but because we never got out at the weekend then we had to go twice. We never wanted to go but the House Masters threatened us that if we did not go then we would be moved to Rathgael which was the Protestant version of St Pat's. One day we were sitting in Mass when we noticed that everytime some-one got up to do a reading the Priest sat down on a wooden chair and although we were not experts we figured out from our woodwork classes that the said chair was held together by screws. After the service we set our plans into action. That Friday we 'borrowed' a screwdriver from woodwork and later that night we sneaked into the Chapel to remove the screws but the screws were star head and we had a flat head so mission aborted. The following Tuesday we put the screwdriver back (told you we had only borrowed it!) and borrowed a starhead. Once again it was a midnight sneak into the Chapel and every single screw holding the chair together were removed – the Wednesday service had now become something to look forward too!

Come Wednesday morning we were in Chapel like a shot to secure a good view. Now I must point out that the usual priest was a young chap so the fall from a chair shouldn't do much harm to him. That's were the first problem arose. He had decided to go on holiday and the priest that replaced him for this service was what we described as a 'coffin dodger' – we were doomed. How were we going to explain a deceased priest! We realised that we were going to have to say something but as we were making our plans we each received massive slaps to the back of our heads and were told to shut up. I can tell you now that that service was the longest ever and when someone got up to do a reading and the elderly priest made his way towards the chair then our fear turned to absolute panic but none of us were going to make a move to warn him because if we had it would have been worse so we hoped that it would not fall and if it did then we hoped that it would seem like one of those accidents. If it had been the younger priest then this would have been brilliant as when the chair was sat on it basically exploded underneath him – I can tell you it was the funniest thing I have ever seen and me and my chair sabotaging comrades burst out laughing when we realised the priest was still alive. Big mistake. We were grabbed outside and lets just say what happened next should have involved the bleed'n Peelers. The Brothers knew instantly that it was us and they made us pay for it.

After our beatings we were taken to the gym which was next door to allow the Chapel to clear and then we were brought in and made to sit at the back pews with about ten feet space in between us. We were covered in blood from our busted noses and a few of us even had black eyes. We were there for hours when the same elderly priest appeared and went into the confession box. Unknown to us we were to confess for what we had done to the very same priest that we did it too – now how difficult do you think that was! I was last and when I went in I realised that I was the one taking the full rap – all the rest had blamed me. Now I must come clean, it was my idea but I did not 'borrow' the screwdriver nor take the screws out. It was a team effort but when the rest of them were in with the priest the word team was lost on them and they blamed the lot on me. When I went in things took a dramatic change. "You must be young Baker?" the priest asked as soon as I got in. "Yes Father," I replied before going through the proceedings. Now there are many things I can do but lie to a priest was not one of them and to this day I reckon I was the only one that told the truth in confession that day. At the end of it the elderly priest told me that he had said Mass in many places around the world but that today's Mass would be the one he would always remember. He saw the funny side of it – it's just a pity that the Brothers outside did not share his view!

One on going case I know of is the kidnapping of a local Derby County supporters beloved rug by the evil Four Bottles of Old English Brigade

Now I know that there are going to be Catholic readers who are going to be horrified at that story but remember I was only thirteen, the priest saw the funny side of it and we all got a pretty bad beating. Practical jokes are great and if it helps we were non sectarian in carrying these out as the best one ever involved King Billy, some red noses and one hell of a dangerous climb. Some people assume that because I am now this respected writer, community worker and all round good guy that I seem to have grown out of all this stuff - yeah right! Practical jokes are absolutely brilliant and do have this unique way of bringing people together in their planning and carrying out. Now over the years I have heard of some cruel pranks being played but I can state that mine were never too bad. In fact the worst I ever did was screwing a mates front door shut who lived in the high rise flats in the New Lodge but he had covered all my windows in this yuch which he mixed together in his kitchen.

Another kidnapping which I have heard about is actually on going but I have absolutely nothing whatsoever to do with it! In the New Lodge area there is, believe it or not, a Derby County supporter and one of his most prized possessions is a Derby County mat. One day he

was doing a spot of spring cleaning and decided to scrub his mat and leave it out to dry. This was observed by a local terrorist unit of the Four Bottles of Old English Brigade (not to be confused with the splinter faction known as the Two Bottles of Strongbow Brigade). They arranged with one of their crack commando units to kidnap the said mat which, so I hear, they carried out quite efficiently. The mat was then handed over to their military wing, photographed and a list of demands were then sent to the distressed owner. Now because the owner is a relative of mine he showed me the photograph and their list and I have to admit that they are quite a demanding lot. They even asked for four packets of pickled onion crisps and four cans of Coke (one regular and three diet) – now–how could you give in to that! Needless to say the owner refused to give in and the last I heard was that he is now receiving post cards from all over the world from the said mat which, for some reason, seems to have embarked on some sort of a world tour. The last I heard was that it was in Amsterdam but I wouldn't know because, as I have pointed out, it's nothing to do with me!

Another old time favourite is getting people to deliver letters to different places and asking them to get them signed. These started in The Recy and I have previously covered it but there were many other letters and people have been sent to all sorts of places including the old favourite where they are sent to a bank to get a letter stamped. Once the letter is opened it states that the person needs money badly and that if they don't get it they are going to take off all their clothes, sing the Sash and dance naked in the middle of the floor. Now there are people reading this thinking that no one could be that stupid but take my word for it when you get the right person to ask them to go and think of an excellent covering story the rest just falls into place. I remember one person stating that they would never fall for anything as stupid as that. A few days later they were standing in a local clinic with a written note requesting information on how to have sex!

Never, ever state you will never fall for anything like that - its just putting out a challenge and even I wouldn't be as daft to state it!

Hello Mr Bank Person

For obvious reasons I don't want to give my name but I have a bit of a problem which you could sort me out with. I have to meet a new boyfriend tonight and to be honest I have absolutely no money. Here's what I want you to do. Please hand over £100 and I will leave. If not then I'm going to take off all my clothes and sing the Sash in the middle of your floor waving my knickers around my head.

Sorry about the big writing but you look like a bit of a thick prick.

Thanking you in advance

Hi

My name is ▓ and I have a bit of a problem. I have started dating a girl and the basic thing is that we really need to know how to do it, if you know what I mean. Because we have never 'done it' we asked a friend to bring us back a DVD from Amsterdam but to be honest we found that extremely confusing as we don't know at what point you introduce the inflatable sheep and whipped cream.

Some time ago I was informed that if you are your girl are 'at it' and she sneezes then the both of you will be stuck together. To be honest I don't want to risk this happening and need to know how to get out of this situation if it occurs.

Could you please give me some leaflets and booklets on how to do it and could you also make them pretty basic as we are beginners. I also understand that you give out special willie shaped balloons. Can I have some please?

I have to do this in writing as I am scared of anyone overhearing.

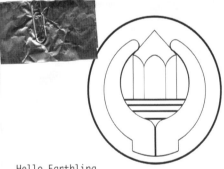

Hello Earthling

My name is Arleneya from the planet Zxctyp. I have travelled for 290,0000 light years to reach your planet in order to teach what you refer to as men to do it properly if you know what I mean. However, I have run into a bit of a problem.

I need to get back to my planet and I was hoping that you can make all the travel arrangements for me. The reason I have come to you is that I have been informed that your office is full of moonbeams so am I to assume that you have crafts in store.

The one which I had was basic but excellent. It had warp drive, protective shield, defensive cloaking device, multi level scanners and fluffy dice on the rear view mirror.

It is my understanding that you earthlings use a system called money. We do not use that but the nearby planet of Ghtyjk has this system. Please find enclosed two Ghtyjk Dollars which are the equivalent of about £10,000 of your pounds. Please keep the change.

Hi

My name is ▓ and I have travelled the whole way up from ▓ to use your services. I don't want to beat around the bush so I will get straight to the point. What I want is a smear but a smear with a difference. I want you to get your youngest, fittest male nurse to smear whipped cream all over my naked body.

I hope you can squeeze me in as soon as possible

Thank you

The bottom line is if you are ever asked to hand deliver a letter treat it with suspicion. Now I have just been made aware of these letters and have no connection whatsoever in sending people with them!
Top left - to the bank. Left - to the Travel Agent. Above - to the local Clinic

GLENRAVEL AND ASHTON

For the past twenty years two of the most important aspects of my life have been the Ashton Centre and my local history work. It would therefore seem unusual to write about these two together but the reason for this is because both developed at the same time and as a result of each other.

Reading the past chapters it is clear that deep inside me somewhere was an interest in local history, which was just waiting to come out. As a youth I remember small incidents such as being upset when beautiful buildings were torn down and when rows and rows of streets in the old Docks area where cleared away. Of course then I didn't know it but what was happening was generations of history were being destroyed and replaced by the ugly greyness of urban motorways. Then there was reading the inscriptions in the local cemetery as we drank cider and another of our past times

which was 'hookin' around in old houses and buildings and to this day I still have old photographs, maps, gasmasks, ARP bells, badges, whistles and fire pumps which otherwise would have ended up in the bull-dozers bucket.

My real interest in local history began when I 'obtained' a book called As I Roved Out from the library (alright I nicked it!) This was a collection of short stories from all over Belfast and I think I just constantly read it over and over. At around the same time I went back to the old records kept in Clifton House on the cemetery and began to copy them. First I copied all the grave-stone inscriptions that were originally compiled in 1909 and then I updated them to what's there now. Then I moved onto the Registry Books and because they would have been extremely difficult to copy by hand I decided to photocopy them.

As all this was going on I still had to work to earn a bit of a living. This was the doom and gloom of the eighties so there was not a lot around. Like most of the district the dole was the only option and I was no different but after a number of events the dole was hit on the head.

A friend and I signed on every second Monday at Corporation Street but there was a problem. This meant that the Peelers knew where to get you if they wanted to and in my case they often did. However it was another Peeler related incident that was to see the end of me ever signing on again. Both of us had just signed on and were making our way home along York Street. Suddenly a van pulled up and its side door opened. A number of men jumped out with boiler suits on, balaclavas and Heckler & Koch machine guns. It was an RUC anti terrorist unit. They screamed at us to get on the ground and spread out our arms and legs. One had his foot on my back and another was on my friend. They held us like this for a few minutes and never said a word the whole time. Suddenly they jumped back into the van and drove off at speed. Both of us lay on the ground staring at each other and, thinking it was a set up, never moved. Slowly we turned our heads, saw that the van was gone and that there was no one behind us. We then got up, dusted ourselves down and then simply walked on. After that I decided that I would never take the chance of signing on again and I never did.

I was very handy with my hands and made a few quid doing small DIY jobs around the area such as putting in new lights, sockets or just wiring up

a cooker. There was also the gardening so with everything combined I was making enough to get by every week. Then a friend of a friend got me some work which to be honest was so enjoyable I think I would've done it for nothing and that was setting up heavy metal concerts in the King's Hall. What this was was the unloading the massive lorries of different bands, setting up the stages, doing security during the concert and then packing everything away. It was very, very hard work but well worth it as we were paid a fortune. Some of the bands I worked with included greats such as Iron Maiden (above), Bon Jovi, Def Leppard and quite a few I'd rather forget about. However this was the best work I ever done as music is the one thing in my life I couldn't live without. Punk and Heavy Metal was always my thing but at the time I'm writing this I am listening to Prodigy but half an hour ago I was listening to Duffy. It's the same when I'm home. I have speakers into my bathroom and therefore lie in the bath listening to music. One night I would be listening to Black Sabbath and the next time classical. I would still love to work at the bands today but to be honest I really don't think I would have the energy for a fifteen hour shift!

The first office of Ashton on the Antrim Road with some of the original committee members. To the far right is Gerry Doherty and fourth from the right is Seamus McAloran

It was at this time that a new group was established in an office on the Antrim Road called the Ashton Centre Development Limited and they, as far as I was aware, were the only community scheme within the area with a photocopier so it was there that I spent hours copying the old registry books. The main person behind the Ashton scheme was Seamus McAloran who was a local community worker and publisher of what was then the New Lodge News. Seamus's work fascinated me especially the publishing bit and it was from then on in

The Apple Macintosh Classic. It's hard to believe that my first publications were compiled on this!

that I became involved with Ashton. It was Seamus who took the time to show me how to work a computer and to do this he must've had the patience of a saint. It was at around this time (mid 1980's) Apple Macintosh computers became available with a ready installed publishing programme and I tried to learn everything there was to know about them. Everything was trial and error and when I made a mistake I learned the hard way not to do it again as I had to start all over again. It was then that I decided to work on my first book and it was to be on Clifton Street Cemetery.

As fate would have it a number of things began to fall into place. Using the old Apple computer was proving quite difficult as it had a really tiny screen but soon after they brought out another that had a much larger screen and if I was to do this book then one of these had to be obtained. At one of the meetings at the Ashton office I got talking to two people from the old Belfast Action Team (now Belfast Regeneration Office), Ritchie Warburton and Carol Bailey. They informed me that it was they who funded the restoration of the cemetery and that the icing on the cake would be a book on it. The problem was they could not fund an individual and it had to be done as part of a project. At that time I was still strongly connected to the Recy and asked the community worker there if I could set up a local

Ritchie Warburton

history scheme and base it in the Recy. She approached the City Council and they said no so the next obvious choice was Ashton. There I asked the committee and they had no problem whatsoever and I have been there ever since.

A few of us then got together to set up this project which was only to publish this one book on the history of the cemetery. It was then called the Clifton Street Cemetery Local History Project. I have no need to point out that this name is quite a mouthful so we decided to change it. The next name was the Ashton Local History Project and because Ashton was named after one of the old streets it was decided to name the group after one, which was or had been closer to the cemetery. The street on which the cemetery was situated was called Henry Place so not much luck there with a name but beside it was another old street, which had once contained a number of buildings of historical interest. This street and all its beautiful old

The old Belfast Mercantile College (later High School) which stood on Glenravel Street

Clifton Street with the old Benn Hospital and Glenravel Street to the right

buildings ranging from the Belfast Mercantile College through to the Benn Hospital was completely destroyed to clear the way for the Westlink Motorway. Its name was Glenravel Street and therefore the Glenravel Local History Project was born.

At the same time things really began to move with Ashton and work began on the proposed building on the site of the old Ashton Street. This new building and scheme was to address the problems of unemployment in the area at a time when things were really bleak to say the least. Because of this I worked away tirelessly on getting this cemetery book completed and the Belfast Action Team had approved a small bit of funding to obtain a new computer to do this. This was around 1990 and in 1991 both the book and the Ashton Centre were completed.

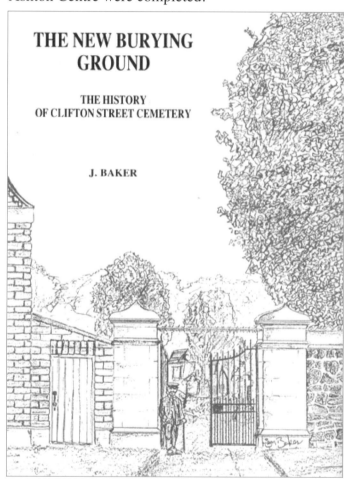

As mentioned the publishing of the book was to be the completion of the project but I then began to get new ideas for additional schemes now that I had the means to carry them out. Shortly after this Paul Steel, who was manager of Ashton, introduced me to another user of the centre called Micky Liggett. Micky was also interested in local history mainly centered on the Bone and Ardoyne areas of North Belfast. Over the next few years both of us were to compile books on the New Lodge, Ardoyne, the Bone, the McMahon Family Murders and even one of old Belfast ghost stories. We then went on to bigger projects and were the first to compile a publication on all those executed in the Belfast Prison on the Crumlin Road.

The proposed Ashton Centre and the actual Ashton Centre

We continued with our local history titles and began to publish titles that focused on true local murder cases. We had looked at English titles such as True Detective and wondered why there were none for the Irish market. Now there was and this was our first title that was distributed all over Ireland. This caused a bit of a storm and it was covered in almost every local newspaper and even international titles such as *Esquire Magazine* but how many would guess that our efforts were reported in the *Guardian* and the *Sunday Times* in the same week!

Using the profits we then purchased more computers, computer programmes, printers, scanners and everything else we needed. We then went on to publish a new magazine called *Historical Belfast* which became the *Belfast Magazine* and eventually *Old Belfast* and which continues to this day. We also developed a new community newspaper first for the North Belfast area and then for the whole of the city. These were free newspapers but we had decided to start a new newspaper which was to be a bought weekly for the North Belfast area and which we were to call the *North Belfast News*. We had advertised this in our free North Belfast paper and the *Andersonstown News* informed us that they had the exact same plan with the exact same name and then approached us. Because they had a lot more newspaper experience than us and were community based we decided not to go ahead with our plans and to allow the *Andersonstown News* to go ahead with us concentrating more on our local history titles. Looking back there are quite a few developments which we were the first to do and which no other publisher was doing at the time. The first was computerized colour printing, which was not developed by us but was only being used by us. At that time we used the *Newsletter* for our printing and we were shocked to learn that we had to print out everything for them instead of just printing from a disk. The second was the use of barcodes and we were the first to use these among the local mainstream newspapers and magazines. We were also the first community-publishing scheme to use a professional distribution company. As for the internet – guess who was using that first in this field?

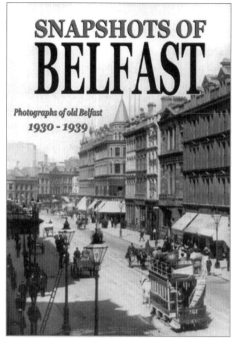

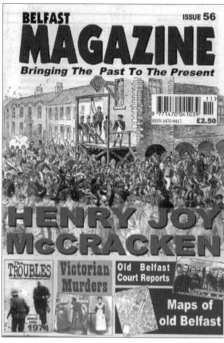

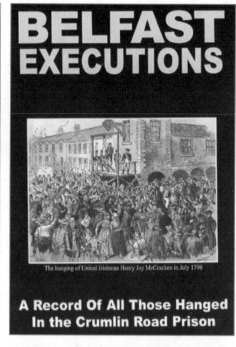

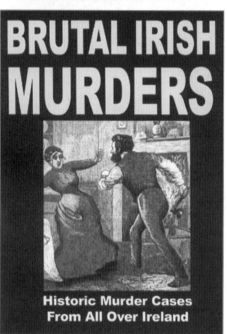

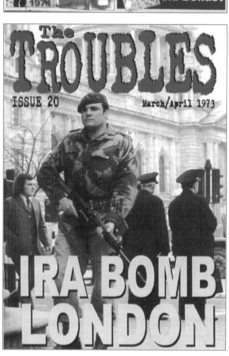

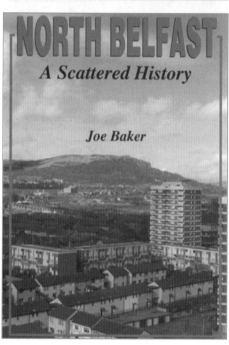

We have gone on now to compile almost three hundred local history titles with an average of twenty being added to that number each year. I myself also compile local history articles in the *Andersonstown News* and *North Belfast News* and compile a local crime feature first for the *Belfast Telegraph* and now for the *Sunday Life*.

Of course there are lots more interesting features to this work. Through the Heritage Lottery Fund we have put together massive photographic exhibitions which we later discovered were the biggest ever displayed in Ireland as well as developed historical walking tours – years before the local Welcome Centre was even heard off. Today there are tours of the old Belfast Prison run through the local tourist office which but one thing I would hate to think is that the City Council paid anyone to develop these and the reason for this is we had developed a DVD from tours we conducted almost ten years previously which are virtually word for word from our accumulated research on the place and its previous residents

We still conduct specialist tours of the prison that are so popular they are at any given time are booked up six months in advance. One thing that I can assure you of is the following. When I was lying in my cell in A2 Cell 20 I can tell you now that the last thing in the world I thought that I would ever be doing would be walking tours in the very building I was banged up in!

Looking down A Wing.
My cell is the open door on the right

Back at Ashton I have to say that things were not going so good. The main aspect of it, the supermarket, had failed as it did not reach the expected turnover. This led to a lot of in-fighting within the Ashton board. To say that these sometimes got a bit heated would be an understatement. Every meeting developed into a massive argument and at times even came close to punches being thrown. Most of the Board had turned against Seamus McAloran and because of the pressure he left. I was loyal to Seamus and had no confidence with the current board and plans were made to have it removed. The only way to do this was through an extraordinary AGM. It was my feeling that Ashton was losing its community base and the only way to sort that out was through the community itself. The board of Ashton was made up of shareholders who were the people, through a community share scheme, who had paid towards the Ashton idea. Sadly a lot of them had cashed in their shares and just walked away but fortunately most did not. I approached the secretary and chairman of the board and instructed them to call and extra ordinary AGM. Before I did this I obtained a full list of the remaining shareholders and went and visited all those I could find. I told them what was going on and asked them to come along to the AGM. Most of them did and it was from then on in that changes began to be made. The chair asked for a show of hands for the board to be voted back on block but none went up. He called again and suddenly one person put up his hand and proposed that the board be voted back on. Now in fairness to this bloke he hadn't a clue what was going on but fortunately no one else backed his proposal. The chair was then forced to vote members on one by one and the only people elected were myself, J.J. Magee and Geordie Boyd. The chair was disgusted and addressed the meeting by stating "control of the Ashton Centre is now in the hands of Joe Baker, Geordie Boyd and J.J. Magee." He was not a happy man. A few days later an emergency board meeting was called and we were back to the arguments. Some of the members resigned and soon after Paul Steele resigned as centre manager. This was bad timing as a few weeks after that I was to leave on a community project in which I was to take ten kids from the New Lodge and team up with ten from Tiger's Bay and ten from Drogheda to go to Maastricht for three months. I know I was leaving J.J. and Geordie in the firing line but I couldn't let all these kids down.

New board members needed to be found and found quickly and now so was a new manager. Things looked really bad for Ashton and I can state that the whole place really did come close to closing down. Some of the board members decided to stay and see it out and in my absence J.J., Geordie and members such as Phil Nichols, Rosin Donnelly and Gerry Doherty began the slow process of recovery. An advertisement went out for a new manager and to cut a long story short it came down to two people with one of them being Paul Roberts who was the best person for the job and just like myself, J.J. and Phil he has been there ever since. The board also got its act together and reorganized with Gerry Doherty becoming the new chairman.

Because of my commitment in Holland (which was an Ashton project I must point out) I missed out on all the fun but one thing I must state is that these were just disagreements on how the Ashton Centre was to run. My loyalty was to Seamus McAloran but thats not to say that I had any resentment towards those who disagreed with me. Of all those who left I can state that I am still friendly with them all and would never pass any of them on the street. We disagreed on the running of Ashton – so what! No big deal and certainly no need to fall out over it.

On my return there was a bit of reorganizing to be done from the top down. The board became more active and because Gerry had other commitments he had to stand down as chairman. The board had faith in me and I was elected. We reorganized the board and Paul reorganized the senior staff. He appointed a new girl called Ciara Connor as his assistant and since then we have never looked back.

Ashton was now getting back to its community base and has went from strength to strength. In recent years we have opened a new childcare centre on the Cliftonville Road and a whole new complex on Henry Place overlooking the historic Clifton Street Cemetery. We now employ well over one hundred people so despite all the arguing and in-fighting it all turned out to be worthwhile.

Of course there are much, much more but with the twentieth anniversary of the Ashton Centre coming up in 2011 I'll have to leave Ashton's history for that!

Ashton's new complex in Henry Place from Clifton Street Cemetery

HEARTACHE AND JOY

In all this time there was also dramatic changes in my personal life. When I began all this work I lived with my wife and two children in a small cramped flat at Alexander House in the Barrack area. Over the years we moved first to a flat on Cliftonpark Avenue and then fixed up what was basically a derelict house in St James's Street just off the Antrim Road. After that we moved to a bigger house on the Cavehill Road.

Just like myself my wife had decided to self educate herself she decided that she wanted to do was go into childcare. She completed all the courses and went one-step further and even learned sign language. Of course we still had our children David and Charlene and when we moved to the new house both were still at school. David attended Hazelwood Integrated School and Charlene Our Lady of Mercy on the Ballysillian Road. When we lived in St James's Street my wife decided to contact her mother whom she had had no contact with for decades as her mother had separated from her father when Sadie was just a child. I helped her do this and looking back it is one of the sorriest things I have ever done for reasons I had better not go into but lets just say we didn't agree religiously or politically! In our new Cavehill Road home everything seemed to be going well for both of us. We had a luxury house, my wife had passed her driving test so we were planning to buy a new car and both children were settled into their schools. From the outside all seemed well but deep down it was far from it.

I know you can never blame things on a house but it seemed as though our luck began to change from the moment we moved into it . One morning our phone went at around five o'clock in the morning. When it woke us Sadie got up to answer it and I looked across and thought mum's dead. I had no reason to think this as I was speaking to her the night before and she had a touch of flu and besides that all was fine. When that phone call went I instantly knew that my mum had died but I have absoloutly no idea how. I got up and was starting to get ready before my wife was able to turn round and tell me what was up. We then had the dreadful task of telling the kids before I set off down to my dad. For those who have not experienced this yet please, please take my word for it that it is the worst feeling in the world. Shortly afterward I told a close friend that I would give anything just to have five minutes with my mum and when his mum died he said to me that he knows now exactly how I felt. My mum and I had always been close because I was the baby of the family but believe it or not I hardly shed a tear. I watched my brother crying and remember thinking there must be something wrong with me because I wasn't

doing it. Apparently it was some sort of delayed reaction as a week later I broke down and cried my eyes out and it really felt like someone had torn my heart out.

This was some bloody start to the new millieum as ten days into it mum was to pass on. I suppose in a way we were lucky because at the height of her drinking she was operated on and given the last rites several times – that was twenty years previously. As is tradition family and friends went back to the local bar (in our case the Rocktown under one of its new names) and there my son David said he was going for a walk. We decided to let him but what he really did was went to the house, packed all his stuff and moved in with my dad. I didn't know about it, his mum didn't know about it and my dad certainly didn't know about it.

That was to remain the case for the next couple of years and to be honest I'm glad someone was with my dad as I know for a fact that being alone would have killed him in a matter of weeks. Sadly dad lost another companion but this time it was his mutt. Finto was a jack russell who was completely thick because he would have fought anything. One day he took on two Rottweiler's in the Waterworks and on another he came in almost completely torn to bits after he and about twenty other dogs fought over a bitch. Needless to say Finto went missing and dad was totally gutted. Now when we were growing up dad was getting every dog, cat, gerbil and hamster we ever owned put down every week but the fact of the matter was he loved them all really. His favourite of all time was our oul mutt Jason. Like all dogs Jason got old and when the council van came for him we were all gutted but dad was devastated. Finto replaced Jason and now a replacement for Finto had to be found and had to be found fast. A friend of mine, Anya Connor, had told me that there was a pup if I wanted it as the person who was to get it had died. I agreed to take it on dad's behalf and left it down in his flat as a surprise when he was down at Tesco. Unknown to me dad came back to his flat and the pup had climbed into the rubbish bin. Dad didn't know what the hell to do but his first reaction was that there was a rat in the bin and to grab a cricket bat. Fortunately he didn't and when he looked inside he was introduced to his new companion – Sparky.

Dad was only to enjoy Sparky's compaiship for a few weeks as one night David was to go into the living room and dad was lying dead on the floor. David didn't know what to do but he ran for help next door and when some of the neighbours came in they did what they could but dad was long gone. And so one of the New Lodge's most well liked and respected characters had passed

One of the last photographs of dad taken at the renaming of the tower block

away. I know that anyone can and will say the same thing about their dad but Charlie Baker was without doubt one of the areas most loved characters and now he was simply no more.

Our Cavehill house was really beautiful but when I looked at it I realised things needed changed and plans were put into action. One day my wife got up with travel arrangements left on the bathroom sink with me knowing she would be in there first. This was a paid trip for her and her sister and a few of the kids to go to Cyprus for a two-week break. Needless to say she was over the moon but this was only a small part of the plan and was designed to get rid of her. Off she went and when she did so the builders and decorators moved in. While she was away every window was replaced, a new kitchen put in, new wooden floors, a new dining room and almost all the furniture in the house replaced. The whole place from top to bottom was redecorated and the garden, which surrounded the house, was landscaped. It's hard to believe but all this work was completed about two hours before my wife arrived home and I thought she would have been absolutely over the moon when she arrived. When she came in she looked at the wooden floor and made a comment on the tacky oilcloth. She then went through the living room with its new furniture, past the remodelled dining room and looked at the new five grand kitchen and exclaimed, "It'll do." That was the beginning of the end.

Another development at that time was our decision to undertake foster care. We had taken in a young girl named Lorraine who was from the Irish Republic and who was blind. Lorraine came from a strict Church of Ireland family and because the establishment she was in was taken over by the Roman Catholic Church her family thought that unsuitable. Needless to say the only option was to send her to a special needs school in the North and because of the travel involved it would be better if she was placed with a family also up North. We became that family and Lorraine was a child I was to become really attached to and really loved.

The relationship between my wife and I was simply no longer existent. Now like any break up there is always going to be accusations and counter accusations and I could now present my case in a fully one-sided way. This I won't do other than to say that the break up was non violent nor confrontational. I had been working in the office in our house when my wife came in and asked if we could talk. I said no and she asked did I want her to go. I said yes and that was that. The following morning I got up and my wife was gone and we were never, ever to speak again.

David was still living down in dad's flat and Charlene was still with me. Letting Lorraine go was the most heart-breaking aspect of all this and as I left her out to the school pick up I kissed her knowing that that was the last I was ever going to see her again.

My son David (third from right - second on march) had joined the Irish Army

The situation I was in now was a single parent with a teenage daughter and believe me that wasn't easy. I was still living on the Cavehill Road but now more than ever I wanted to get out of this house. I realised that there was no way I could get a new place as when the divorce came through that would've meant my wife would have been entitled to half of that. I put the house up for sale for only £90,000 and I knew I was cutting off my nose to spite my face but to me it was well worth it.

David had been living on his own in my dads flat and while there he decided to embark on a life changing decision. He joined the Irish Army. This was a major pick up as I have to admit that his passing out parade was one of the proudest days of my life. Charlene got herself a new place and began a new job at Tie Rack so for all of us things were begining to work out ok.

I was not to stay single for very long as I was to meet a girl not at a pub, work, niteclub or even on line dating but at a funeral!

Myself and Micky Liggett went to the reinternment of Kevin Barry in Dublin and stayed overnight. While there we met up with a group from the Bone and among them was Anne Turley. Anne's husband lived in the housing estate facing our flat in the Barrack but when they married he had moved up to the Cliftonville. Mixie, her husband, died and Anne was now a widow. That night in Dublin nothing happened but we all had a drink together, went to the funeral the next day, got soaked to the skin and went home.

A few weeks later I met Anne again at a function organised as part of the New Lodge Festival. A few days after that we went on our very first date and through our ups and down we have been together ever since. We ended up married on the 6th of October 2007 and for that we decided to plan something that little bit special. I had proposed in St Stephen's Cathedral in Vienna and then got the engagement ring in the diamond capital of the world – Amsterdam. The engagement ring was then put on at the stroke of midnight at the new years party on Dam Square. Plans were then made for the wedding and because we were engaged in Amsterdam we thought we had better get married there which we did. We brought over our immediate families and married in St Nicholas Roman Catholic Cathedral. Now in case your wondering how I was able to remarry within the Catholic church then the answer is simple. My first marriage was in the City Hall Registry Office and therefore not recoginised by the Catholic church. We then went to Moscow for our honeymoon taking the new Mother in Law with us! On our return had our reception. Not your everyday normal wedding but for such a special day we decided to do something special and this was it. Of course some may think that all this cost a fortune and it did but look at the cost of a normal wedding and ours had a similar price tag so why not do something completely different!

With the new wife came new children and even grandchildren. Anne had three children to her previous husband, Leeann, Michael and Anthony so when people now ask how many kids I have I think they're a bit gobsmacked when I say five and five grandchildren. Anne and I had so much in common that it seemed natural for us to end up together and the one thing that we both had was a deep urge to travel.

BROADENING MY HORIZONS

There are two things I enjoy today and they are history and travel and quite often I combine them both. When I'm away I like to look up the history of the place and quite often I visit these places because of their history. The other thing I do is look at all the history from both sides such as the wars For those of us who have been to Milltown Cemetery we will be well aware of the graves situated there of the IRA (both Official and Provisional), the INLA and of the various other republicans scattered throughout it. But how many of us are aware of the graves situated there of the victims of World War One and Two? In Milltown there is the large cross of sacrifice memorial and the mass grave of the victims of the Belfast Blitz. There is also the line of graves of six polish airmen and numerous commonwealth graves of individual soldiers who were killed and buried here. Across the road at the City Cemetery it is a similar story. I began a series of visits to the battlegrounds where a lot of these soldiers lost their lives and it is something which I would highly recommend anyone to do. These days there are many tours organised which visit the sites of famous battle-fields and sites throughout Europe and further afield. Having been to a few I can tell you that at times they can be quite moving and even frightening. For example when you visit the site of the Somme you can't help but be moved by the senseless loss of life and imagine what it's like at Volgograd (Stalingrad) where thousands of human bones can still be seen lying around till this day.

Some of these battlefield sites can also be very frightening. For example at Stalingrad thousands of human bones still lie scattered in remote areas.

My first trips began in Paris and then by bus or to the sites themselves. One of the most interesting places to visit is Ypres in Belgium. The first thing that strikes you about this place is its outstanding beauty and although it looks so old it is hard to believe that this town was completely destroyed by the Germans during the First World War. When the war ended the town was not only rebuilt but was rebuilt exactly as it was. In its centre is the old Cloth Hall which now houses a fascinating museum on the First World War and this is an absolute must see for everyone who visits. It is also in Ypres where my favourite bar is situated. I can't remember its exact name but it was something like Black Death (serious!) and behind the bar was Satan. Now before you think Satan was the ten foot tall Hell's Angel type barman it was actually his dog. I don't know what type it was but it was

The Menen Gate in Ypres where a memorial service is held every night

The old Cloth Hall in Ypres in which the museum is based

massive and looked as though it was sussing you out for its din dins. Now you would think you would run a mile from this but this is where false perspectives once again come into it. Although painted black the bar had a great atmosphere and was very comfy. The barman was extremely friendly and kept bringing us down snack after snack and as for Satan the dog - it was actually a big kitten which was constantly looking petted!

Every night at Ypres they hold a memorial service to those who lost their lives and in the battlefields around this town and we are talking tens of thousands. Visiting the cemeteries and walking among the thousands of small white headstones was one hell of an experience and when you begin to read the headstones your thoughts instantly turn to outright pity when you read the ages of many of those buried here including one 14 year old Irish kid who must have seen it all as one great big adventure.

Of course many Germans were killed also and I went around a few of their cemeteries such as Langemark where over 44,000 lie buried and Menin (47,864) and these also proved quite moving. For example at Langemark I was shown a small plot of land no bigger than the area of an average house which contained the remains of over 25,000 German soldiers. To be honest I think that it is quite important to look at both sides of each story and in this case I learned that extreme suffering occurred on both sides. Nearby is a large garden dedicated to all the Irish soldiers and to be honest I never realised that there were so many killed. There is also a large stone tower 32 meters high representing all 32 counties of Ireland. Near to this is a small tearoom known as Hill 60 and this is more of a museum than a tea room. Out the back is a large room filled with items which are still being recovered from the fields around it. These include everything from helmets, badges, bullets, bombs, rifles, machine guns and don't ask how, but the biggest sea mine you're ever likely to set your eyes on! Out in the back field is the Hill 60 trenches which are extremely well preserved and

although we could never imagine the horrors which must have taken place within them, they really do give us a bit of an idea of the conditions which they must have had to put up with.

Then I went to somewhere where I never, ever thought I would set foot on - the Somme and on the way I learned a lot about the actual German trenches. While their British counterparts were holed up in muck piles a lot of their trenches were made out of concrete, had electricity and running water and even bedrooms!

The Battle of the Somme, fought in the summer and autumn of 1916, was one of the largest battles of the First World War. With more than one million casualties, it was also one of the bloodiest battles in human history. The Allied forces attempted to break through the German lines along a 25 mile front north and south of the River Somme in northern France. One purpose of the battle was to draw German forces away from the Battle of Verdun; however, by its end the losses on the Somme had exceeded those at Verdun.

Verdun would bite deep into the national consciousness of France for generations, and the Somme would have the same effect on generations of Britons. The battle is best remembered for its first day, 1 July 1916, on which the British suffered 57,470 casualties, including 19,240 dead — the bloodiest day in the history of the British Army. As terrible as the battle was for the British Empire troops who suffered there, it naturally affected the other nationalities as well. One German officer (Captain von Hentig) famously described it as "the muddy grave of the German field army." By the end of the battle, the British had learnt many lessons in modern warfare, while the Germans had suffered irreplaceable losses. Looking at these trenches today you can't help but wonder what it really must have been like and also to ask ourselves - did we really learn anything from it?

Pachendale Cemetery

The Blue Mosque

Haghia Sophia, the oldest church in the world

These graves were not the first I had ever visited as a few years previously I had taken part in a project to Holland. A few miles outside Maastricht in the Southern Netherlands I went to one of the American graveyards and the amount of headstones within it really is disturbing. In May 2009 friends of mine who are involved in the Connaught Rangers Association invited me to visit the war sites and graves in Gallipoli in the European side of Turkey which most of us would be aware of through the Mel Gibson film although it didn't point out exactly how the Australians treated the Irish soldiers. It was here that many thousands lost their lives during the First World War with casualties being from Britain, Ireland, Australia, New Zealand, India and of course Turkey. Turkey was on the side of Germany and they had defeated the allies at the Gallipoli Peninsula many of whom had been killed before they had even left their ships as these had come under bombardment from massive gun emplacements dotted around the coast.

As mentioned this trip was arranged through the Connaught Rangers Association as it was this regiment that was almost completely wiped out here. The trip began in Dublin with a flight to Istanbul and I'm afraid that when I arrived there I was totally distracted as the history was so unbelievable. Here I was actually standing in Constantinople which was to have become the capital of the new Roman Empire and although only here for one night I had to explore and take in as much as I could.

Emperor Constantine and Empress Zoe at each side of Christ at the Haghia Sophia

Quite close to my hotel was the famous Blue Mosque and what a building. This really was something else but at 5am when the call to prayer was blasted out over massive loudspeakers my admiration for it somewhat disappeared! This mosque is situated in beautiful surroundings filled with fascinating history ranging from actual Roman and Egyptian monuments through to the famous 'Million Stone' where the whole world was to have measured from. Facing the Blue Mosque is the Haghia Sophia, the supreme church of Byzantium, which, despite being over 1,400 years old, is still in a remarkably good state. The interior is absolutely breathtaking. Nearby is the Baths of Roxelana, the Basilica Cistern where you can see the marble head of Medusa (the one with the snakes for hair) as well as the Hippodrome where the Romans held their chariot races and no doubt fed the odd poor souls to the lions. This was on one side of the Blue Mosque and on the other was a small Bazaar where salesmen try to sell you everything from luxury rugs through to the usual tacky souvenirs. I couldn't believe it but one of these Turkish salesmen actually spoke Irish!

The following day it was a very early start for our long five hour journey to the Gallipoli Peninsula which was fascinating as here we were driving along a road in Europe looking across into Asia! Our destination was the small village of Kocadere where we stayed at a complex known as the Gallipoli Houses which was a beautiful complex designed as a number of self contained apartments. Ours was absolutely beautiful with outstanding views but sadly it had a bit of a down-side. At the back we had our own patio but less than fifty feet away I spotted our early morning wake up call - the local mosque. Now in Istanbul the call to morning prayer was very, very loud but only lasted a few minutes but our new found country version was to have its own unique ways. When the call went out by loudspeaker at 5am the local dogs joined in with their howling and when all was complete the local rooster population (of which there were quite a few) began their cock a doodle dooing which went on and on and on and on. Now reading this book you will be aware that I hate cruelty to animals but you take my word for it if I had had my way here there would have been a mass slaughter of roosters and I wouldn't have cared less how they would have met their end!

As for Turkey itself there were quite a few misconceptions I had with the main one being that it was made up of sand and rocks but it was far from it. It was almost as green as Ireland itself. The beaches were absolutely beautiful with crystal clear water washing up on to the shores - quite tempting for a swim if it weren't for the bleedin jellyfish!

Another misconception I had was that the place was full of mosquitos and I myself prepared by bringing loads of cream and repellent spray because if anyone was going to get stung out of our group then it was going to be me - it always is! Anyway one night when I was in the land of nod I woke up with the buzzing of a fly type creature close to my face. Grabbing my spray I jumped up and went into battle with my spray can. Having secured my victory (there was no more buzz-ing) I turned on the light and discovered that I had nuked a normal everyday housefly and left the room like some-thing out of Chernobyl.

The purpose of this trip was to visit the battle sites and

The wooden horse which was used in the film Troy and which is on display at Channakale

war graves throughout Gallipoli but for one day we took a break from this and travelled over to the Asian side to Channakale and from there to the ancient city of Troy. Now this was a surprise to me as I always thought Troy was in Greece but then again totally thicko here thought that Gallipoli was in Italy! When we arrived at Troy we were met with a massive reconstruction of a wooden horse, the story which I'm sure most of us are well aware. Anyway this got me thinking about how history could have been so different if another decision had been made. What if, I thought, that instead of coming out and bringing the wooden horse into Troy full of enemy soldiers one of the Trojans said "I know - lets burn it!"

That didn't happen and Troy was destroyed and today standing among the ruins you cant help but be amazed at the scenes of history you get there. Here I was standing in a place which I had learned about in school, read about in books and of course seen in the famous Brad Pitt film and I really couldn't believe it. We had a tour guide who told us all its history and if you are planning a future trip here then make sure you do it with a guide. Imagine what it's like being told all the stories and legends of Troy while standing in the middle of it - it really is something else even if you have little interest in history.

Leaving Troy we headed back to Channakale where the wooden horse used in the film Troy is on display. Getting on the ferry we left Asia and headed back to Europe to continue on our battlefield tours. This time we headed to Suvla Bay. Now most of us will never have heard of it but for the music buffs among us it is mentioned in the song "The Band Played Waltzing Matilda"

The band played Waltzing Matilda
When the ship pulled away from the quay
And amid all the tears, flag waving and cheers
We sailed off for Gallipoli
And well I remember that terrible day
When the blood stained the sand and water
And how in that hell they call Suvla Bay
We were butchered like lambs to the slaughter
Johnny Turk, he was ready, he primed himself well
He rained us with bullets, and he showered us with shell
And in five minutes flat, we were all blown to hell

To be honest I think this section of the song tells the story better than I ever will but it gives us an idea of what it must have been like. Most of these soldiers were slaughtered on the beaches and looking at the outstanding beauty today it's hard to imagine how this place could be described as hell. It was then time for another hike and we went around the memorials and battlefields at Anzac and Lone Pine where there are preserved trenches and tunnels. When hiking everyone finds items such as bullets, shells and various other bits and bobs of war related items - that is everyone except me! What was my amazing discovery which would get me onto Time Team? The top of a food can! After our hike it was back to the bus and therefore back to our hotel. This was the final day of our tour around the Dardanelles and what a tour it was. These sites were the final resting places of tens of thousands of Turkish soldiers who died defending their country and over 30,000 British and Commonwealth soldiers who died trying to take it. For me it was a very moving experience.

That night was a chill out one with a few local brews outside under a clear night sky. While chilling out with everyone else one of the serving Irish Army soldiers pointed out another first for me and like the dolphins at Eceabat it was something I had never seen in my life. Turkey borders with Syria, Iraq, Iran, Armenia, Georgia and across the Black Sea Ukraine and Russia and because of this it attracts a lot of international attention. Looking up we watched numerous satellites going across the night sky and because of the direction they were going the military blokes among us were able to tell us which were American and which were Russian but for me it was just an amazing sight.

It was also while we were chilling out that I discovered another bit of information - we were setting off to Istanbul first thing the next morning- and I mean first thing!

The most impressive war memorials that I have ever seen have been those erected by the Russian's. The Soviet memorial facing the Reichstag as well as the massive one at Treptow Park would have impressed anyone who has visited Berlin. The most impressive of these memorials are to be found in Russia itself. For example in Volgograd (Stalingrad) the war memorial of Mother Russia (above) is the largest freestanding statue in the world. There is one in Moscow known as Victory Park and words simply fail to describe it. On entering you are met with massive water fountains on each side and then standards commemorating different sections of the Soviet army, navy, air force and people. Straight ahead is an enormous bronze monument, which must be at least two hundred feet high, which is moulded from top to bottom with scenes from all the major battles fought between the Soviets and the Nazis. Behind this is the building itself and on entering you are met with a large hallway completely covered with Soviet flags and standards as well as, surprisingly, a massive bust of Stalin. You are met with a large staircase, the central section of which brings you up with the side sections going down. Deciding to go downstairs first I discovered that this was the section dedicated to all the Soviet people who died in what the Russian's call the Great Patriotic War (World War Two).

The first thing that strikes the visitor is the ceiling, which is made up of millions of hanging chains. Finding this strange I had to make inquiries and was told that each link represented each person killed. With Soviet losses being over 26 million then it gives you an idea of the size of the place. This section of the memorial was made up of long corridors and at each side were thousands of books containing the names and details of each person killed in beautiful handwritting. I also learned that the page of each book is turned every day. There are also thousands of photographs of civilians being killed and tortured by German troops. All were extremely disturbing but one that stuck in my head was of a little girl being raped by Romanian 'soldiers,' and that is now an image, which I will take to my grave.

Due to the unusual shape of the building each corridor leads you back to the central staircase and then it was upstairs to the section dedicated to the military. All around are numerous cabinets with artefacts from the war ranging from letters right through to massive bombs. Once again there are hundreds of Soviet flags but at the end there is one extremely interesting section. Here the floor is glass and underneath are hundreds of Nazi flags, standards, armbands and even iron crosses and the idea here is that you walk over them as a sign of disrespect. At the end is the story of the siege of the Reichstag and on display here is the actual flag the Soviet troops flew over the German parliament. On leaving this section you go up to the next level which is a large art gallery and a real impressive one at that. On entering you are met with massive Soviet and Russian flags and then various paintings and art pieces. Lots of the paintings are war related but there are quite a few religious works as well as numerous Russian subjects. Next to this is a small section in which paintings by local school children are put on display, which I thought, was an excellent idea. One interesting section I found fascinating was a display stating why this will never happen to the Russian people again. In it is a make up of the Russian

On display here is the Soviet flag that flew over the Reichstag

army, air force and navy, the type and amount of nuclear missiles at their disposal. Basically what they are stating is that they could quite easily destroy our planet. Another part explains why they were forced to do this and have stated that their arsenal is in response to that of NATO.

On leaving this building you are then directed to a major outside section which shows everything from World War Two tanks right through to modern jet fighters. If there are any future plans to come here the one bit of advice I would give is make it a whole day as there really is a lot to see and take in. As I have previously mentioned this place is covered from top to bottom in Soviet material and you would be forgiven for thinking that it was built in Soviet times. This is not the case as this was built in 2005 and was designed to reflect the modern thinking in Russia. As mentioned elsewhere many people in Russia now realise that the grass was not greener on the other side after all and a sign above the entrance to the Victory Park says it all:-

We live in a time that follows the collapse of a vast and great state, a state that, unfortunately, proved unable to survive in a rapidly changing world. But despite all the difficulties, we were able to preserve the core of what was once the vast Soviet Union, and we named this new country the Russian Federation
Vladimir Putin

There is absolutely no doubt that Moscow is our favourite place to go and the evidence of this is in the amount of times we have been there. What's unique about here is that every time we go we are always doing something different due to its sheer size. Of course there's the Kremlin and St Basil's (left) but there's a lot more. Those which spring to mind range from the All Russia Exhibition Park (above) through to the Cosmos Museum (below) which shows all the stuff about space and presents the evidence that the Soviets stuff America in the space race. The first time we went we booked ourselves into Hotel Russia which was a small complex of only three thousand rooms overlooking the Kremlin. We went in May for both the Commie parade on the 1st of May and for the Victory Day parade on the 9th of May. The commie parade was held in Revolution Square and here there are quite a few speeches given out to the faithful but it is also a wonderful place to go to see all the old veterans.

One of those I bumped into had fought during the Second World War and stood proudly with his Soviet flag and portrait of Stalin. He saw my hammer and sickle tattoo and gave me a traditional Russian kiss as a mark of respect. Now the man was about ninety and the traditional Russian kiss was a smack on the left cheek, then the right and then a massive smacker on the lips - that was bad but suddenly it was to get worse. He then called his wife over and she did the same thing but she was older. Not only was this a parade I was never going to forget but these were kisses I was certainly never going to forget in a hurry.

However the most impressive parades are those, which take part on the 9th of May to commemorate the Soviet victory over Nazi Germany. These take part in Red Square and are the most impressive parades I have ever seen in my life. These are very much communist affairs and involve thousands of Russian troops, vehicles, tanks and the odd nuclear weapon, any one of which could be the beginning of the end! Many of the soldiers carry the standards of the thousands of Soviet regiments and as they march along they sing what I assume are Russian marching songs. At the beginning of the parade they are dressed in the uniforms of the Second World War as a mark of respect to the veterans who are all seated at each side of Lenin's tomb. At the same time large speakers on the Kremlin walls are

blasting out some sort of a chant and the whole thing is actually quite intimating but totally fascinating. We tried to count the soldiers at one time and got ten across and one hundred along so that was a thousand troops in each section and there were hundreds of sections. The weird thing I remember thinking was that they all seemed to be the same size but I have no doubt that this would be more to do with paper stuffed under their helmets rather that a very strict recruitment process! At the conclusion of the parade giant planes and helicopters fly overhead followed by formations of fighter jet planes that are flying so low you can actually see the pilots.

At the other side of the Kremlin is another sight that must be seen and that is the changing of the guard at the tomb of the Unknown Soldier. (Top right) This takes place every hour on the hour and is really fascinating to watch. Another unforgettable sight is back on Red Square at the tomb of Lenin which is open a few days each week to allow the commies to pay their respects to the founder of the Soviet Union. Needless to say there is a process to go through and no one is allowed in with cameras, bags phones or come to think of it anything other than the clothes you are wearing. All items not allowed are to be left at a building before you queue but here's a wee tip. Go to one of the tour guides, give them the rouble version of a few quid and they will bring you straight to the front of the queue which stops you lining up for hours. You then go to a

security section for searching and that's you through. Once in to the tomb itself there are quite a few guards and quite a few rules. No talking, stopping, hands in pockets or anything that would be disrespectful to Mr. Lenin. On one of our visits I was walking slightly ahead of my wife when out of the corner of my eye I spotted her bless herself. Through gritted teeth I whispered, "did you just do what I think you did?" Suddenly there was a nasty "schhhhhh" from one of the guards.

I then decided to get out and get out quickly. Now when you leave the tomb you can then visit the graves of other Soviet leaders and heroes such as Stalin and Yuri Gagarin but for me it was a hasty rush out and away from those guards. I then asked my wife "what in the name of good feck was she doing blessing her-

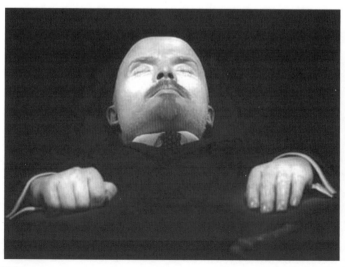

self?" "I just said a prayer" was her response. It was then that panic set in as I realised she must have then blessed herself twice. "Well the guards didn't say anything," she quickly added. To this day I still believe that the said guards are still in shock and are receiving counselling! There are common sense things you don't do in Lenin's tomb such as spitting, calling him a commie scumbag and bloody blessing yourself! Their belief is that religion is the superstition of the masses so any religious mumbo jumbo is a strict no no.

Thankfully a trip to Siberia was avoided but just when I thought things could not have got any worse I was wrong. As I mentioned our hotel was facing the Kremlin and one day we were making our way back to it. Now one problem with Moscow is that there are stray dogs everywhere but they don't do you any harm and I think it's a case of you leave them alone and they'll leave you alone. Having grown up with dogs all my life I know that one thing you never show them is fear. However it was a different case as far as Anne was concerned. As we were going back to our hotel we were forced to walk past about ten of them which were lying on the footpath in the shade of a bus shelter as the weather was a bit hot. I said to Anne to just walk past them as though they were not there and to totally ignore them and walk on. Suddenly when I got to the pack they all jumped up and snarled and barked at me. Something had triggered them and at first I thought I stood on one of their tails. I was ok and just snarled back at them they pulled back a bit. I was more concerned about Anne but didn't want to take my eyes of the dogs. "Give me your hand and come on" I said to her. Total silence. "Anne give me your hand" I repeated and again nothing. Then I assumed the worst and thought Anne had fainted so I slowly looked round. Anne was a dot on the horizon with her running being the thing that triggered the pack and therefore leaving me to get tore to bits. Needless to say they didn't but later when I eventually found Anne I asked her what the hell she ran for and was told, "you would not have got through them because they only understand Russian!" I had only planned to walk past them not open up a series of negotiations.

Revenge was to come soon after as one day we were walking down Stary Arbat, which is one of the main tourist streets with souvenir shops and stalls up and down the street. As we were looking at one of the stalls with its massive collection of Russian dolls and Soviet memorabilia we were approached by what can only be described as two raving lunatics. Anne was the main attraction and they were lifting items of the stalls and giving them to her and taking photographs of her on their phones. To give you an idea on their insanity one of them was running around with a jet fighters helmet on! One of the stallholders decided to call the cops and what do you think I did? Well remember what she done with me with the pack of dogs – sorry wolves? It was my turn to become a dot on the horizon!

If you are ever planning a trip to Moscow there are two bits of advice I will give you. One is to make sure you obtain a visa otherwise you simply won't get past the passport control at the airport. The second is to make sure you check the weather. We had simply assumed that it was going to be cold and packed all our winter woolies and long johns but when we got there it was a bleedin heat wave. The other thing about the place is the sense of being constantly followed and on one occasion when I was with a friend he suddenly turned around and photographed a guy who seemed to be around us everywhere we went. Now if you look at the photograph (below) can anyone state that he is not some sort of FSB (KGB) looking guy!

For some strange reason Hotel Russia was pulled down and is at the time of writing being rebuilt. The reason I say this is strange is because the hotel was perfect and there seemed to be absolutely nothing wrong with it. Because of this we began staying at another landmark, which was the Ukraine Hotel. This was housed in one of several buildings dotted around Moscow known as the 'Seven Sisters' and which Stalin, as part of his plan to rebuild the city, constructed. These buildings are quite unique and today are described as Stalinist/gothic and you either love them or detest them. I think they are fantastic.

Hotel Ukraine (above) was a fantastic building and to be honest I actually feel privileged to have stayed in it. The ceilings are painted with fantastic Soviet murals and the whole building has that unique feel to it. At the lobby there is the main bar and this is open 24 hours a day and working around it are the unique ladies, whom, I later discovered, are in the lobbies of every hotel in the city. When we were at the bar I was totally fascinated watching these women at work and the way the whole operation was being carried out. Once they obtained a client they seemed to go to this one girl and give her what I assumed was money. She in turn went to the reception, collected a key and then gave it to the girl who then went up in the elevator with the client. I was watching out to see how long 'things' took but none of the clients or girls returned so I assumed that the 'bookings' were for the whole night. It was also at this lobby bar that we had one of our strangest drinking nights. Anne and myself had been sitting enjoying a drink when a guy came across and asked us if anyone was sitting on a chair. We said no and he took it across to his friends. A few moments later he came back and asked us if we were from Ireland. When we said yes he introduced himself as one of the staff of the New Zealand Embassy and told us that some people were coming across from the Irish Embassy. Soon afterwards they did and we ended up all drinking together. As it turned out we were having an absolutely brilliant craic when more and more people

began to join our company and all of them from different embassies from around the world. Then an American came over and he was from Texas. Now he just came over and asked could he join our company and because of the way he was dressed we knew he was from Texas – think overweight with cowboy boots and hat. The abuse that man took from us was tremendous but in fairness it was all in good humour and he gave as good as he got. One of the embassy guys started to get really friendly with me and I noticed that he was constantly ordering drinks but drinking very slowly himself and sometimes giving it away. He kept asking me questions about North Belfast and seemed extremely knowledgeable about the whole area. He wanted to know about different interfaces, Girdwood and the general mood of the area. Two could play at that game. Throughout the night I asked him if he was in Moscow long and where he learned to speak the language. He said that neither of them could speak Russian and that aroused my suspicions. If he were to work at the Irish Embassy in the middle of Moscow would it not be a good idea to speak Russian?

We continued talking anyway and his whole interest seemed to be on the feelings of people in North Belfast about different things but to this day I'm convinced that this meeting was a set up. Here we had a guy from the Irish Government who knew a lot about North Belfast who said he worked for the Irish Embassy in Russia but could not speak Russian and was talking to someone who knew North Belfast quite well and staying in a luxury hotel in Moscow. What are the chances of that! When we are traveling throughout Moscow we always use the metro and I would love to be able to describe this to the reader but this system is so fantastic that I can not think of a any words that could do it justice but those I would use would be along the lines of reliable, beautiful, amazing and totally fascinating. Doing what metros are designed to do it is quite reliable with trains every few minutes moving millions of people with complete ease. The stations are really something else as well and instead of thinking of typical underground stations such as those in London you should instead be thinking art galleries because that's exactly what they

are. There are works of art on the walls and the lights are generally chandeliers with seats made out of marble and bronze waste bins next to them. Most of the stations are on different Soviet themes with the main stations having statues of every type of worker imaginable. I myself love traveling on this metro and although I have been on it hundreds of times each journey is a different experience. Now lets just say you were on the London Underground and some guy pulled out a massive machine-gun and began cleaning it. What would you think? Hit the deck and get off at the next stop with a quick call to the cops! In Moscow that is no big deal and thousands of soldiers travel to different bases and use the metro so although someone like me would instantly think this is it, girls next to these people continue reading their books! Staying with soldiers it was also on the Moscow Metro that I saw one of the saddest sights of my life.

At the Victory Parades in Moscow all the remaining veterans are gathered in their uniforms for the main march past of the Russian Army. Once this is over they receive the eternal thanks of the Russian people and are then presented with a large bouquet of flowers by a child as a symbol of thanks for giving them a future. After one of these parades I went on to the metro and when I sat down I noticed one of these very old veterans sitting directly facing me. He had on a white uniform with about twenty medals and was holding his massive bunch of flowers presented by one of the children. I sat looking at him during the whole journey and do you know throughout that whole journey that man sat staring at the one spot on the floor. I just watched him and thought of what that poor old man has been through, what he has seen, whom he has seen killed? Who has he killed? Was he at Stalingrad? Was he at Leningrad? Did he liberate any of the Nazi concentration camps? I had so many questions but sadly he would never have understood a word I said and I would never have understood his replies. When I got off the metro I stood and watched the door closing and the old veteran disappear down the deep tunnel to his stop never to be seen by me again. During that journey I wanted to just say thank you but it's only now that I know it to be SpaSiba. I just wish I knew it then.

Another misconception about Moscow is that the Russian Mafia are everywhere. There's not much I can say about this but to give you an idea of this type of belief it was not all that long ago that people abroad thought that one hundred bombs were going off in Belfast each day and that everyone was running about with a gun ready to kill anyone who looked like a Catholic/Protestant.

Our local in Moscow is the Shamrock Bar on Novy Arbat. Now for those who know me the first thing I always condemn Irish tourists for is their urge to go to Irish bars when they can go to any number of them here.

While abroad I have only ever met one Irishman who ran an Irish bar and that was Rocky in Prague. They are usually run by people from Scotland or England or just by people who sell Guinness and stick a tricolour up. In Moscow there are quite a few Irish pubs and believe it or not there is a St Patrick's Day parade. We had arranged to go to that one day but the temperature fell to minus 30 so we decided to give it a miss. Back to the Shamrock, there are two reasons I go to it and that is the fact that they sell Harp and the second is that the food is absolutely marvellous. I have no idea who owns it as I have not yet met him or her but what I do know is that it is used quite regularly by the Russian Mafia types. They come in well dressed and looking quite dodgy, sit at their tables, eat and drink and cause no problems whatsoever. I have sat feet from them many times and never has there been any concern. Mind your own business and go about doing what your doing and why should there be!

Being a regular I have worked out why they come here. The bar is part of a huge shopping complex with one way in and one way out which is quite open and wide with no way of being able to come up the stairwell unseen. When the Ruski Mafia types come in their bodyguards sit in the corridor outside and simply watch everyone coming up the stairs. Obviously they know who they're looking for as not once has Anne or me been stopped by them or harassed in any way. Just as well as I would've hit them a good boot in the arse and sent them home. (In my bloody dreams!)

Here we would be sitting feet away from the god-fathers of the Russian mafia sipping our drinks so would it be possible to make things any more risky. What would you think if I told you that my dear wife sips tea with the Taliban? Well every time we go to Moscow this is something she does quite regularly. Like Hotel Russia the Ukraine Hotel has also closed for a major refurbishment. The place we stay now is the hotel complex built for the Moscow Olympics (top right) and next to this is the massive market situated at Izmaylovsky. It is said that the Grand Bazaar in Istanbul is the largest market in the world but having been to both I would state that its Russian version is twice the size. My wife, as a professional shopper at my expense, would agree. At Izmaylovsky you can buy anything from a Kalashnikov to a Koran and its sheer size really is something else. There are two parts to it with the first being the section that sells millions of Russian dolls, dodgy DVD's, t-shirts, a flea market and the odd gun dealer. The second part sells everything from so called fake handbags, purses, watches and clothes from the worlds leading retailers. Now the reason I say 'so called' is because the same people who make the genuine articles in China are also making these 'fake' goods that are sold throughout Russia. Now if the same people are making the same goods, using the same materials and the same workers then how are they fake? The multinational companies are not endorsing them – so bloody what! Anyway my beloved is a handbag freak and she spends hour upon hour going up and down the several miles of stalls that make up this section of the market. Most of the traders are from China and most of the goods come from there but there are quite a few from places such as Afghanistan. Most of these dealers are people who fought against the Soviets and who are now fighting against the Americans. When I am out doing what tourists do my dear wife is off shopping in this market and quite often she stops at the odd stall and sits and has a cup of tea with the Afghans and shares stories. Once the Afghans find out we are from Northern Ireland they are fascinated and ask question after question. Their hero is Michael Collins and they described him "as the pebble that brought down the cliff." On a few occasions I got to speak to them about what was going on at present in Afghanistan and most of them now seem to accept that what the Soviets were doing was wrong but that they were being used by the Americans. They also state that there are sections within the Russian military who are covertly supplying them with hi-tech military equipment and who are getting their own back on the Western involvement in the Soviet/Afghan conflict.

My wife has her friends at this market and I have mine. She goes into the clothing, handbag, watch and shoe section and talks to the people she talks too. I go into the flea market section and talk to fascinating characters ranging from stamp collectors through to neo Nazi moonbeams that have all sorts of genuine Hitler type memorabilia on sale. This market is what it is all about. Here we have hundreds of different people from all over the world with different religions, cultures and politics. The one thing that unites them all is the fact that they are prepared to work to earn their living. These are the people Marx, Engels and Lenin talked about and who are the true working class – those who work.

If Moscow is our favourite city there there is no doubt that Amsterdam is the most special. The first time I had ever went to Amsterdam was when I was part of the Wider Horizon programme which saw us bring thirty teenagers at a time to the Netherlands for three month placements. The kids would be placed with a family and also placed in a work scheme in Maastricht (above) which was in the south of the country between Germany and Belgium.

Not all the kids stuck it out but for those who did we took them up to Amsterdam to enjoy their last two nights. There was only one basic rule and that was no drugs and not to even think of trying to bring any back. We had stated that anyone stopped at the airport would result in everyone staying and their parents having to pay to get them home. Sounds a bit tough but experience taught us that sometimes a joint would be placed in one of the others bags without their knowledge and that this was done for a laugh. The young people really enjoyed Amsterdam as it was one hell of an eye opener for them but there were also the surprises. Amsterdam is known throughout the world for it's red light district but who do you think were the worst behaved in it – the boys or girls?

Needless to say the boys were in like a shot walking up and down and eyeing up nearly every girl. This did not last long as after about an hour they got bored and simply went to the nearest amusement arcade. The girls were really something else. They were up and down every street, lane and alleyway as well as in and out of nearly every sex show!

In addition to the red light district Amsterdam is also well known for its drug scene and although I have been there countless times with different people these are two things which have never appealed to me. Now I know there are people reading this thinking 'yeah right' but I really do mean it. Amsterdam is a real beautiful and relaxing city and is perfect for that chill out city break. There are numerous museums, galleries, markets and plenty of shops but the one thing I enjoy the most is the walks along the canals. These are everywhere and when out on a stroll you completely lose all sense of time and while you think one hour has passed it would really be several.

I have been there many times with friends with each having its own unique experience. On one of these my friend Junior and I went only to discover that we had no hotel. We ended up staying on what can loosely be described as a boat as it was barely afloat and had the smallest beds I have ever had the misfortune to try and sleep in and in the smallest cabins. So here were were staying on a very, very old boat which was slowly sinking and had tiny beds in tiny cabins. Just when I thought things couldn't have got any worse then I had Juniors snoring in the next cabin through paper thin walls and Romeo and Juliet on the other side doing their stuff. Amsterdam is the first city Anne and I visited together and it was also here that I got engaged, had my stag party, had our wedding rings made, got married and it is here that we come every Christmas and New Year. Christmas is the one time of the year that I utterly detest and every year I watch numerous friends dig themselves into deeper debt. I really do hate it and that is why I am one of the few remaining members of the Bah Humbug Society. This time of the year is just full of hypocrisy and to give you an idea of what I mean then I'll use the words of one of my favourite authors Sevn Hassel. He was a German soldier during the Second World War who wrote about his experiences in the 1950's and 60's. In his book *Liquidate Paris* he states the following:-

I wandered down the Vesterbrogade. Behind each window was a little tree or little lights or pretty paper baubles. Happy Christmas! Happy Christmas every-one! The catch phrase on people's lips. Happy Christmas, merry Christmas. Just a catch phrase, nothing more. It didn't mean a thing. You try knocking on a door and begging for a mouthful of Christmas goose and you'd find yourself on your arse in the gutter before you knew where you were.

Can you tell me he's wrong! In Amsterdam Christmas day is just like any other and they do not celebrate it on December 25th but earlier in the month. Because of this all the shops are open and everyone goes about preparing for Europe's biggest new years eve party at Dam Square (below). Anne and myself go to this every year and then make the journey home on the first day of the new year.

St Nicholas's in Amsterdam where Anne and I were married

It is also in Amsterdam that we enjoy our shopping trips both to the well-known stores and to the markets. There is a nice big market in the city next to the city hall and it is well worth a visit if ever you go. The place is also home to quite a few bars and night-clubs. These range from the quiet pint jobs through to the dope smoking madhouses. Now I'm not a dope smoker but I have nothing against it and believe it should be legalised to take the criminality out of it. Anyway during one of my earlier trips with a group of friends we decided to go into one of these madhouses and try the odd joint. We were given a list but looking at it we hadn't a clue so we called over a waiter type chap and asked him what was what. We ruled out several before we came to ones that made you laugh. He gave us the name and told us to go to the bar and to take one every half hour. Up I went and, as there were five of us, asked for five of these joints. Back I went to our seat (well mat on the ground) and lit up. At first there was nothing but a bad smell and a headache but after about twenty minutes one of the group said he needed to go to the toilet and as he tried to get up we all started laughing. Every half hour I went up for five more and we really did laugh the whole night until, quite a few hours later, the waiter type guy came over and asked us what the hell we thought we were doing? We were meant to take one every half hour – but one between us!

If someone had come in a told us our families had been killed in a horrible earthquake we would have laughed because by this time we were laughing at anything. The next morning we paid for it because leaving aside the thumping headache and the sore jaws the laughter line across our stomachs was in total agony. I never smoked another joint again in my life and I don't think all the ones with me have ever touched another either.

In Belfast I have my local bar and that is the Duke of York in the old Half Bap area but in Amsterdam I also have my local and that is The Bottle. This is a night bar and stays open till about four in the morning. I have been in it so many times that I am on first name terms with all the barmen. Anne and I have made many friends

in this bar and all of them from all over the world. We've drunk with Iraqis, Iranians, Americans, Russians and people from all over Europe and there really is nothing like it.

Another great thing about Amsterdam is because of its rail network you can be in any part of the country within an hour or so. In addition to this you can also go to Germany, Luxembourg and Belgium within a few hours. There are many who believe that Amsterdam is the capital city of the Netherlands. It's not as it's The Hague, which is just under an hour away by train. We go there quite often to shop in the local market, which is one of the biggest in Europe.

In addition to the market people set up stalls in the streets, which surround it and that's where the real trinkets can be picked up. There are quite a few things to do in The Hague but the most fascinating is what they call the miniature village. This, as the name would suggest, is a huge collection of Dutch landmarks in miniature. It is really fascinating and the work that must have gone into it is really remarkable.

It was also from Amsterdam that Anne and I carried out one of our most unique trips. We arrived in Amsterdam and spent one night in a hotel and told them we would be back six days later. We then went on a massive train journey not really knowing where we were going and having nowhere booked to stay. First we travelled to Maastricht and spent the night in one of their snobby hotels because you get them cheaper if it is a very last minute booking. The following day we crossed the German border and stayed in Aachen. Again we crossed the border and this time to Brussels in

Aachen

Brussels

Rotterdam

The railway station at Antwerp

Belgium and then up to Antwerp. Antwerp is a real beautiful city but the place I found the most impressive was the railway station and this really needs to be seen to be believed. From there we entered back into Holland and this time to Rotterdam. This city is fascinating and is a real hi-tech modern city as most of it was destroyed during the Second World War. It also has a massive Irish connection and it would seem that most of the ex pats have settled here. After a night here it was back up to our hotel in Amsterdam and back home to Belfast.

Reading this you could be forgiven for thinking that I never go anywhere in Ireland but of course that's not true. One of my favourite places on this planet is a small village called Callan which is a few miles outside Kilkenny. This village is not much to write home about but it is so relaxed and easy going that it is the perfect place to 'get your head showered' to use the Belfast expression. It is surrounded by monasteries that were totally destroyed by Oliver Cromwell and is a shocking example of the suffering Ireland endured at the hands of English rulers.

One of my favourite cities is also Dublin but the problem with here is that it's just to bloody expensive. Now there's not a lot in Dublin I have not seen but sadly a few of my Dublin traditions are being erased. For years I always went to Glasnevin Cemetery and placed flowers on the grave of Michael Collins. At that time it seemed that only me and one other unknown person were doing this but since the making of the glamorised film the grave of Collins is completely covered in flowers constantly. Michael Collins was always a hero of mine and this was long before the film came out. I have had many an argument on the subject and on one occasion punches were thrown. In terms of politics the man was set up by DeValera but I don't believe DeValera set him up to be shot as I think he died during a general attack on Free State troops and that the anti treaty forces of the IRA did not know Michael Collins was in the ambushed convoy.

Anne and myself then decided to concentrate on the grave of another Irish hero and that was Anne Devlin who was the housekeeper of the United Irishman

Robert Emmett. The suffering this poor woman went through was unbelievable and her whole life was a tragedy. For years it was Anne and I who went to her grave every time we were in Dublin, cleaned it up and lay flowers on it. Now it is well kept and other people are now beginning to lay flowers. In August 2009 we were part of a tour to Dublin and Anne spoke at the grave of Anne Devlin and everyone there were almost reduced to tears.

Now for those who are going to think that this tour was a bit biased then I simply must inform you that you are wrong. On that tour were Catholics and Protestants, Unionists and Nationalists as well as ex members of the IRA, INLA and UVF. Yes the tour visited nationalist shrines but it also went to the main British war memorial in Phoenix Park and were told the stories of the Irish regiments who fought in the First World War before flowers were laid at the memorial altar.

While I love visiting Dublin I also love going to London and this is due to the simple fact that there is so much to see and do. I have lost count of the amount of times I have been to London and I have seen everything from Buckingham Palace right through to Number 10 Downing Street. I have went on countless historical tours in the city ranging from the London Blitz right through to London's most famous resident Jack the Ripper. I simply can't get enough of the Imperial War Museum and as for Anne – she has this thing about Tower Bridge and must go to it on every visit.

Anne and I also enjoy the shows in London and these have ranged from Wicked right through to Mama Mia but the best was undoubtedly We Will Rock You. I think we have went and seen this at least four or five times and as the years pass us there is no doubt we are going to see it a few more times more. Naturally Anne and me have had our moments in London and the most unique was when we were getting off a tube and the doors closed leaving Anne on the train and me on the platform. I stood waiting as I knew Anne would have the sense to get off at the next station and come back. Now don't pick me up as being racist but as I was standing there I noticed that everyone was looking in my general direction and that they were all a different colour from me. I moved back to the wall of

I have also read up on his history and today can tell you quite a bit about it. For example if I were to ask you where St Stephen's Tower was in London what would you say? Well before you Google it you might know it better as Big Ben. I really do love London history and all the stuff on Victorian Britain so while I have some people calling me a Fenian so and so earlier now I have others calling me an out and out Brit lover!

There is one thing I really hate about London and that is some of their statues. For example the statue of the infamous 'Bomber Harris' needs to be guarded due to the fact that it was constantly being attacked due to his war 'activities'. Yet at the Houses of Parliament there is a statue to Oliver Cromwell whose crimes, especially against the Irish, are simply beyond belief.

The grave of Karl Marx

the platform and of all the sections of wall I could've stopped at was written some graffiti that said "Kill All Whites." Talk about feeling uncomfortable! I realised I would stand a better chance if I made it known I was Irish and every single person who came within a ten meter radius got a quick "Top o' the mornin' to ya ba Jases."

It is also in London that one of my shrines is situated and that is the grave of a hero of mine. No trip to London goes without a visit to the grave of Karl Marx in London's Highgate Cemetery and while Lenin may lie in permanent state in Moscow this is the true central spot of world communism so stuff your Bomber Harris and Oliver Cromwell's – on this grave is a statue of a man who really left his mark!

Talking about people who left their mark, it was in London that I met one of my hero's. Sadly it's at this stage I have to admit to being a bit of a Trekie. Now please allow me to point out that I was never into the first series with Captain Kirk and all the moving boulders but more into the Next Generation and all the stuff that followed. One day Anne and I were walking through the West End when I spotted this guy and pointed out to Anne excitedly "there's yer man off TV." Anne hadn't a clue and asked what was he out off. Was it Eastenders. The Bill? No I screamed. I was struggling to remember his name but not his acting name but his real name.

"It's Will Riker from Star Trek, bloody Number 1" was what came out. At this stage Anne went running after him and I sort off stayed behind. Suddenly his name came to me and I caught up with Anne and told her "Jonathan Frakes. His real name is Jonathan Frakes." It made no difference because Anne was straight up to him asking "excuse me mister – are you out of Star Trek?" "Yes" he said and before another word could be said I was over like a shot. Mr. Frakes (Number 1 to fellow Trekies) seemed to be more delighted that we knew him and knew his real name than we were of him. I didn't ask for any autograph or photograph but just said hello and informed him that I thought he played a great part in Star Trek The Next Generation and that I really enjoyed his Thunderbirds movie. He was so over the moon that he offered us to come along with him up to the playhouse where Patrick Stewart was playing a part in a West End play. The timing was bad and we said that we had to meet up with friends in an hour and get our flight back to Belfast. One of the biggest mistakes of my life. What I should have said was "no problem, lead the way and stuff my friends and stuff my flight back to Belfast – I'll get the next one." For non-Trekie types Patrick Stewart played the part of Captain Jean-Luc Picard in Star Trek the Next Generation. To make matters worse my favourite story of all time in either book form, play, film or TV drama

is Charles Dickens's Christmas Carol. My favourite actor ever to have played any part in any adaptation of this was the very same Patrick Stewart!

Jonathan Frakes (standing) who played Will Riker in Star Trek. To the left sitting is Patrick Stewart who played the role of Captain Jean-Luc Picard

Growing up there were two places I had always wanted to go and the first was Moscow with the second being Berlin. Not only have I achieved this dream but have been to both quite a few times. As you would expect Berlin is a modern city as most of it was totally destroyed during the Second World War but there are still fascinating things to see and do. I remember the very first night staying there being woke up by Anne who was screaming for me to get up as they were evacuating the city. Outside there were thousands of people going along the road at speed with police cars flashing and helicopters flying. This was late at night and when I got up and looked out I couldn't believe what I was seeing. As it turned out it was a roller blade marathon. If I had looked out I would have said something along the lines of "c'mere till you see all these people" but no not the girl I married. She had us under nuclear attack leaving me with the slight problem of trying to get asleep afterwards!

There are also fascinating Soviet things to see in Berlin with one of the main ones being the Russian graveyard facing the Reichstag. In this are buried the thousands who tried to storm that building and who were met with extreme German resistance. Today its a large

monument which includes two T34 tanks and cannons which it is said where the first into Berlin. Note I stated 'it is said' because to be honest I don't believe that bit because if these were the first Soviet tanks into Berlin then how come they weren't blown to bits? Anyway leaving aside this slight disagreement it really is impressive and well worth a visit.

Leaving this monument will bring you to the Reichstag itself and one of the things that impress me most about this building is the fact that they were able to restore it. This building was totally destroyed in the war yet looking at it now you wouldn't think so much as a stone was thrown at it. A short distance away is another amazing piece of restoration work – the Brandenburg Gate. It was also across the front of this that a section of the infamous Berlin Wall went and although long gone the road is still marked to show where the wall stood. On the subject of the wall then here's a wee bit of a warning to any future visitors to Berlin. All over the place there are people and places selling genuine

bits of the Berlin Wall. These are in bags and are bits of concrete with paint on them however that's exactly what they are! The first thing that will strike you is that the paint is spotless, fresh and bright and every bit of the wall has this paint. What about the sections of wall with no paint and the sections on the East German side? In addition to this why is the paint so clean? I think you can see where I'm going with this and that is that a few enterprising Berliners have mixed up a bit of concrete in their back gardens, let it set then cover it in different colours of paint. It is then broken up and sold to unsuspecting tourists. To be honest I think it's a brilliant idea and has me thinking of setting up a stall at Castle Junction where you can buy your 'genuine' brick from the Belfast Peace Line and if you buy two you get a free IRA bullet cartridge!

Because of my love of history I always go out of my way to find out a bit about the places I go to and this is doing a bit of reading up before I go and talking part in walking tours once I'm there. In Berlin I decided to go on the Nazi one and although you can always expect a bit of exaggeration you never expect total out and out rubbish. Don't ask me how this came about but our tour guide was a guy called Kenny from Glasgow and to say his tour was a wee bit beyond belief would be an understatement. To me he seemed more interested in getting into the Russians for what they did in Berlin. There is no doubt that they did indeed commit dreadful atrocities but in war all sides carry this out. Bearing in mind what the Germans did in Russia and the atrocities they committed what did they think the Russians would do when they reached Germany – hand out flowers! We were also told that the word Nazi came from Czech word for filth. Now my German is not the greatest but my understanding is that Nazism is German for nationalism and therefore Nazi would simply be German for nationalist but leaving that aside why would any political movement want to call themselves filth? He then took us to the spot of Hitler's bunker and his rubbish he told was so bad that a couple of Americans butted in and told him so. He had no answers as I think he knew he was talking rubbish. I asked him about the alternative views of what happened to Adolf Hitler. For example I asked him his theory on Hitler escaping. The first into Berlin were the Soviets so if anyone is going to know what happened to Hitler then it is them and if anyone is good at keeping secrets then it's the same Soviets. Ten years after the collapse of the Soviet Union Gregori Parappov, a former KGB agent did. At the Soviet collapse he removed secret papers and took them home so that they would not fall into public hands. These presented the evidence of what they believed happened to Hitler which stated that Hitler double Walter Heim was killed in a plan to convince all those in the bunker that Hitler killed himself and therefore

the people friendly and, most important, the drink cheap! As you would now come to expect there have been quite a few incidents here also and there have been that many I don't know where to begin or even what to include. On one occasion my brother Liam and I traveled by train from Berlin to Prague in a five and a half hour journey. We were to meet Anne who had flown in direct from Belfast. Sitting in our compartment we twisted and turned hundreds of times to try and make ourselves comfortable. Fifteen minutes before the train reached Prague we discovered that the seats converted into beds! On the same occasion when leaving Prague Anne was called by airport security. When asked to identify her case armed security guards held their guns to her head then surrounded her. To cut a long story short Anne had bought me a lighter but it was a lighter in the form of a 9mm Browning and really looks the part. And what did me and Liam do while all this was going on? We sat there and didn't move. We came to Prague from Berlin so pretended she wasn't with us!

On another occasion Anne and I embarked on another five-hour railway journey only this time it was to Vienna. Now I'm going to admit being a total thicko again as I thought Vienna was Venice with its romantic canals and gondolas but as it turned out Vienna was a better choice for what I had in mind. Now to be honest Vienna is too snobby for my liking and too bloody expensive. For example a keyring was fifteen Euros, which is near fifteen quid – for a keyring!

Now that I was in Vienna and not Venice and bit of instant research was carried out on the hotel computer and it was then that I realized that fate had intervened when I came across St Stephen's Cathedral. I'm not deeply religious but Anne is and everywhere we go we always go to religious places ranging from St Basil's in Moscow, the Vatican in Rome and even the burial church in Dublin where the remains of St Valentine are situated. What I had in mind needed to be done somewhere religious and St Stephen's was absolutely perfect.

lead the Russians to believe that. It then presented the evidence that Hitler escaped with his deputy Martin Bormann. Kenny hadn't a clue what the hell I was talking about. Doing historical walking tours in Belfast I gave Kenny one bit of advice. Never, ever treat your audience as though they're stupid!

Moving back to the Soviet theme there is another more impressive monument in Berlin and that is at Treptow Park (above). Once again this is a massive graveyard and what the Russians did here was take all the marble from Hitler's headquarters and build this memorial. There are large tablets at each side telling the story of the Russian 'liberation' of Berlin and in the centre is a huge statue of a Russian soldier holding a German child.

Another first ever thing done in Berlin was a hot air balloon ride. Never, ever, ever will I be doing that again. When it went up my grip got tighter and tighter and I was so rigid I couldn't move a muscle. This was scary and what amazed me was the fact that Anne was talking away to another woman as normal as you like!

Although not one of my childhood dreams another favorite city is Prague. The beauty and history in this place is outstanding and for those who like to get out and about there is a lot to see and do. Once again I have been there many times and the first thing that struck me about the place was that every shop seemed to be selling Russian dolls and Soviet stuff – even more so than in bloody Moscow! The buildings are beautiful,

When we were out doing our tourist type things we 'accidently' came across St Stephen's (above) and in we went. Once inside we sat and admired its outstanding beauty and as we were doing so I turned to Anne and asked "would you get married in a place like this?" "Too right I would" was her reply. "Then why don't we?" I stated. This was my way of proposing without doing the down on one knee thing. Looking back I never got an answer as she just burst out crying but I assume it was yes and we did indeed get married! Getting back to Prague it was also there that I seen the gods of rock – Black Sabbath. I had been there with a group of friends on a stag party and one night I saw something that was very important but when I woke up the next morning (sorry afternoon) could I remember what it was? I knew I had seen something but sadly drinking until five in the morning did have a slight effect on my memory. A few days later I saw it again and this time I wrote it down on a cigarette box and got my photograph taken beside it but I had no need as the following morning I remembered. It was a poster advertising a concert for Black Sabbath. Now I had seen Black Sabbath once before in a reunion concert with Ozzy Osborne in Birmingham but what I think shocked me about this one was that they were still going. Judging by their age and the amount of drugs they must've taken over the years I figured that there was no doubt that this would probably be their last. Now I've been to the odd concert and even worked at

them so I knew all the old tricks. Anne and I went over and bought two cheap tickets that were basically just to get us in through the front door. Once inside the plan was to push our way from the back to the front using any number of tried and tested means. The most common one is the old dark glasses trick where you push your way through pretending your mate is blind. I even have a cousin who took this one step further and who 'borrowed' a wheelchair to get to the front!

Once we were in our plan hit an instant brick wall so to speak. There were thousands at it and when we moved in to begin our 'blind friend' journey we just happened to notice the blokes at the back. They were seven foot tall, built like certain brick houses and had Hells Angels across their back. That was that plan hit on the head. We then stood around and waited on our opportunity and noticed one of the barrier security arguing with someone. This was perfect and we simply bolted through and made our way up to the balconies and enjoyed a quiet evening with Mr. Osborne and Black Sabbath. Having done this type of security before I knew that we never went looking for those who bunked in. What we did was waited at the bar for them to come and get a drink so what I did was simply avoid the bar!

Staying in Eastern Europe another place, which fascinated me, was Poland and to be honest my heart always goes out to the poor old Poles because of the suffering they've had to endure. The Second World War began over the Nazi invasion of Poland and about freeing it. Throughout it the Poles fought bravely in many important battles including the Battle of Britain but their liberation never came. At the VE celebrations they were snubbed and after the war Churchill simply dismissed them and handed control of their country over to the Soviets. The Soviets will point out that they saved Poland from the Nazis which, in a round about way is true, but the when Poland was invaded in 1939 it was by two countries and that was Nazi Germany and the Soviet Union in a pact that was planned to see Poland totally destroyed.

When Anne and I went to Poland we went to its capital Warsaw and saw numerous sights and met numerous people. Some of those we talked to told us about their history and the hatred for the British and Churchill for what happened after the war was made quite obvious. On the other side of the coin our barman at the hotel we stayed in was a commie through and through and told us about how things were during the communist period and that the ordinary people were well looked after through various programmes ranging from work through to healthcare. This was the same story we had heard in Moscow, Prague and East Berlin but when my wife informed him that I was a commie with hammer and sickle tattoos on my arm and leg the free drinks kept coming throughout whole stay!

Having been to Moscow and seen the seven sister buildings I had been aware that one of those had been built in Warsaw and therefore had to be seen. Indeed it was and it was at this building (above) that I was asked the most unusual question ever. At the bottom of this building are numerous statues to numerous workers including a teacher. Anne took extreme interest in this statue and then came over to me nad asked if Lenin's wife's name was Mary. Lenin's wife was Nadezhda Krupskaya but as you would expect I was more than curious where the hell Anne had got Mary from. She took me over and showed me a book held by the statue of the teacher that Anne pointed out said Mary Engels

Lenin. What it did say was MARX, Engels, Lenin as a list of the three founders of communism. Thank god she never had the opportunity to say that in front of Stalin!

While in Warsaw we went to one of the Soviet graveyards and met a gentleman who we had absolutely no way of communicating with. He was an old man and although we could not understand a word he was saying we were able to work out that he was telling us that these soldiers were totally forgotten. When the Soviets pulled out of Europe they had an agreement that all their monuments were to be maintained to the highest standard in Poland this was not carried out. In places such as Germany, the Czech Republic and Hungary this was the case but not in Poland.

This Soviet graveyard was neglected but while I fully understood the Polish reason it needs to be stated that these young Russian soldiers died fighting for Warsaw and more than likely hadn't a clue about the politics of the whole situation.

From Warsaw we took one of our infamous long railway journeys only this time to Krakow. This is without doubt a remarkable place but when we got there without any booking I'm convinced that Anne had done a little bit of internet research before we got there. Allow me to present my case. Upon arrival we made our way to the town centre to go into a hotel and ask if they had any rooms for the night. As we were doing so

Anne with the veteran we met at Warsaw's Soviet cemetery

Anne seemed to know her way about and we walked past at least a dozen hotels before we got to the main square. Once there Anne was able to walk me across the square and point out that this looked like a nice hotel. "Where" was my simple answer at which point Anne pointed out a doorway. Ok it looked like a nice doorway but, being in Polish, there was nothing to say it was a hotel. In we went and I have to agree the hotel was absolutely beautiful and, in Belfast terms, think The Merchant. Just like the Merchant it had a similar price tag so because Anne paid for the hotel in Warsaw then it was my turn so you tell me that wasn't pre planned!

I am aware that a lot of people go to Krakow to visit Auschwitz but this was not the purpose of our tour. The purpose of our trip was to go to the salt mines (top right) and for anyone planning to go there simply take my word for it that this is really the must see place. Basically what they are, as the name would suggest, are salt mines but over the years the workers had carved numerous statues and even built places of worship. Now you would expect these to be small cramped places but the carved Roman Catholic chapel is bigger than most cathedrals. Regardless of your religion or political belief it really does need to be seen and you can take my word for that.

One city which I must point out is well worth a visit and that is Budapest. There is no doubt that it is one of the most beautiful cities and one which has so much to see and so much to do so, if anything, at least you'll never get bored. It is made up of two sections which are Buda to the east and Pest to the west and when both were merged then so was the name. Both are separated by the River Danube which leaves Budapest and Hungary for Austria. There are many beautiful buildings ranging from the Parliament right through to former royal places. Another sight worth seeing are some of the residential areas where plenty of scars from World War Two can still be seen on many of the buildings such as hundreds of bullet holes and shell blasts. Anne and I stayed at a hotel called the City Inn which was close by to a residential area and of course the local bar. Close by was the Central Market Hall which is well worth a visit if even just to see it. Downstairs is the main food market and upstairs is where you can get all your Budapest souvenirs ranging from the usual keyrings, fridge magnets, postcards and plates right through to Russian dolls and Soviet odds and ends. On leaving the Central Hall we are left at one of the bridges which brings us over to Buda.

You never know what you'll see at the Central Market.

Once across we come to the Buda Hills where the famous castle is situated. It's a steep climb but one which is well worth it. The castle and the town surrounding it is absolutely beautiful and the views over Pest are breathtaking. Across from the castle is another hill (and another climb) which brings us to an ancient fortification which was used right up until World War Two and which bears the scars of this conflict. German troops held out here until they were overwhelmed by the advancing Soviet Army and who looked down as the retreating German's destroyed all the bridges crossing the river. There is a brilliant waxworks museum here called The Bunker and no visit to Budapest is complete without going here. The first thing that strikes you about it is the biased view of history and how pro Nazi it is. Everything is centred around the German occupation of the site and the impression I got was that the swastikas flying here were flying with pride. Now I'm not saying that the Hungarians are all a bunch of neo Nazis but it is clear that the owners of this museum are. There are horrific photographs on display of casualties of war and of the atrocities committed but the caption of one of them caught my eye. It showed soldiers fighting in one of Budapest's streets and it's caption was "Hungarian, Romanian and German troops fighting aggressive Soviet invaders. Aggression which was to last almost fifty years. Ok, lets leave out the German, Hungarian and Romanian invasion of the Soviet Union and the deaths of almost thirty million Soviet people.

Staying on the Soviet subject then there is another must see place just outside Budapest and that is Memento Park. When the Soviets pulled out of Eastern Europe all the new independent countries pulled down and destroyed Soviet statues with the exception of Hungary. They removed them all to a large park and named it Memento Park. Here on display are dozens of communist statues of Red Army troops, Marx and of course Mr Lenin himself. There is also a gift shop selling various Soviet items ranging from medals through to mugs bearing a portrait of Stalin. I couldn't resist picking up a spoof South Park poster showing Stalin, Mao and Che Guevara as South Park characters with Lenin lying dead with a hammer and sickle sticking out of his head and the caption "Oh my God – They've killed Lenin.

There is one city on the planet which I thought I would never, ever set foot in and that's Rome. It is hard to believe that there is so much to see and do in just one city but if I were asked to sum the whole place up in just a few words then it would be the fact that you certainly won't ever get bored! We have all heard how expensive Rome is and for many people I'm sure that was the case but if you fall into the usual tourist traps then there is no doubt you will find that that is true.

Obviously all the usual tourist stuff of Rome was done such as the numerous fountains, Colosseum, arches and of course the remains of the Roman Forum and all are well worth visiting especially the Forum as this was the very centre of the Roman Empire and the feeling you get just being there is beyond words. Not only could a whole day be spent here but a whole week as there really is so much to see. On top of this there is the Colosseum which is just outside and then the Arch of Constantine who, with out going into any great details, put the Roman into Roman Catholic.

Staying on the Roman Catholic theme we are all aware that the centre of this religion is the Vatican which is a separate country situated in the centre of Rome. Now regardless of your religion or none this is a place that you must visit. The main place here of course is St. Peter's and if you want to see the Pope himself then Wednesday is the time to go as that is when he comes out to do his blessing in front of thousands who gather in St. Peter's Square. I decided to give that a miss but one place I went straight to was the Sistine Chapel. On the way to it there is the Vatican museum where you will see all sorts of artefacts saved from the Roman Empire and the Egyptian Empire. Here you will see everything from carved marble tables of the Romans right though to the famous Egyptian coffins and mummies which were originally placed in the pyramids. To get to the chapel and back is a four mile walk and every single step will amaze you with the art work of Michelangelo through to the massive carved remains of the once mighty Roman Empire.

Everywhere I go I like to see other sites off the beaten track and I noticed the Roman pyramid which, to me, is a must see attraction. This is a gigantic pyramid built into the ancient walls behind which is the must see graveyard of non-Catholic foreigners of Rome. Here rest the remains of the English poets Keats and Shelly and if someone had said to me that someday I would be visiting their graves then the men in white coats would have been called for!

The Arch of Constantine which is between the Colosseum and the Roman Forum

The art in the Sistine Chapel is beyond belief

Not many people know there is an ancient pyramid in Rome and even less are aware that the famous poets Keats and Shelly are buried behind it

The feeling you get being at the Roman Forum is just beyond words

These are only a few of the places I have been but believe it or not some of the most enjoyable are actually a lot closer to home. I have mentioned that I enjoy Dublin and London but there are other places I really enjoy such as Edinburgh. For those who like their history Edinburgh is a good place to start and I have to admit that for various reasons it is really special to me. Being a lover of history I really enjoyed the tours here. These ranged from the underground city tour right though to the story of Greyfriars Bobby, the wee dog that lay on its masters grave until it died. There are also the Burke and Hare tours, which tell of the two Irish men who took bodysnatching to a new extreme. They cut out all the hard work of digging up bodies and simply murdered poor old unfortunate drunkards and sold their bodies to doctors. Often on trips to Edinburgh a railway journey is made to Sterling and to the old town jail. This is really something else and for those planning to visit Scotland is a must see attraction.

Sterling is between Edinburgh and Glasgow and Glasgow is another place with special meaning with the most recent being a trip to the local hospital. Anne and myself would come here often for the shopping to have a meal at two of our favorite restaurants. On one of the latest visits I developed a slight pain in my back and during my few days stay this pain got so bad that I was forced to go to hospital at around 5am in the morning. Now knowing what local hospitals are like I was expecting a wait of at least three hours but was shocked to have been called within a few minutes and

treated instantly. This pain had got so bad that it really felt like someone had stabbed me in the back with a poker and then twisted it about. I was in agony. The medical treatment I got was second to none and although I spent the rest of my holiday (plus a few days more) stuck in hospital I was extremely well looked after. I'll talk about health stuff later but apparently the problem on this occasion was diabetic related and involved leaking kidneys.

Now although I was going through all this suffering and pain it was nothing compared to what my wife was going through. She had my credit card as I gave it to her to buy me shorts and a t-shirt for the hospital. What she did was buy me the latest brand names when all I wanted was the cheapo stuff out of Primark. However it was also the same card that helped my poor wife get over her trauma, as she had to go and take part in a slight bit of retail therapy. What I was going through was nothing compared to the suffering she endured. Here I was lying in hospital in bloody agony with my wife stuck in a luxury hotel room with my credit card but sadly more suffering was to come. One night my poor wife was out shopping with her newfound friend (i.e. credit card) when she returned to her room. Because there was no fridge she set her bag of Maltesers on the windowsill. As they were there being chilled a massive seagull swooped down and nicked them. To this day the only traumatic event, which occurred to my wife in Glasgow, was the thieving seagull that nicked her Maltesers while her husband lay in agony in a hospital bed.

Now I have been to Scotland many times since and my step daughter even lives there now but have a guess what my lasting memory of this place is going to be!

Glasgow Royal Infirmary which became home for a while!

As I have pointed out several times the two places I always wanted to go to were Moscow and Berlin. Now I have been to both several times this leaves me in a dilemma of where to go next.

Unless I get hit by a bus tomorrow (or today now that I think about it!) I plan to go to Paris and at the time of you reading this the chances of me being there are probably past tense as I have a booking for November 2009. Now I know there are lots to see here ranging from the Eiffel Tower through to the Notre Dame Cathedral.

However my main interest is in the Paris Sewer Tours (above) where you are taken down into the rat infested sewers and shown around. That's different and that's for me. Another two places I want to go bring me back to Russia and the first is Leningrad, which is now known as St. Petersburg (right). The second is Volgograd, which most people will probably know better as Stalingrad. Another dream would be for me to travel across Russia from the European side right through to the Asian side. From there I would travel down to Australia, as this is the place of another life long hero

of mine – Ned Kelly (bottom left). This dream will only happen if I win the lottery so if I ever win twenty million then I will give 99.% of it to help those less fortunate but I'm sure I would be forgiven for splashing out just a wee tiny bit on myself but don't hold your breath if your waiting on these travel stories! Staying closer to home there is one dream I have not yet achieved and that is to visit all 32 counties of Ireland. At the time of writing I have been to eleven of them so I guess I'm getting there. When my wife Anne and I discussed this we planned to fly to Cork and visit the sites of another hero of mine, Michael Collins, who was born and shot dead there. The plan would be to then travel up back to Belfast and that is something we plan to do real soon unless I get hit by that mysterious bus that is!

GOOD LUCK, BAD LUCK AND MY LUCK!

There is one place you will never see me and that's the bookies. You'll be glad to know that there is quite a good reason for this and its nothing to do with anti-gambling principles. It's down to the simple fact that I must be one of the most unluckiest people on this planet.

What I'm about to tell you is a strange story in itself but take my word for it when I state its absolutely true. I only do a bet on Grand National Day and a few years ago I had a bit of a weird dream before the said race. I had dreamt of putting a bet on a horse and it winning and when I told people of this occurrence it was like being quizzed by the Gestapo. I was asked everything from what the horse's name was right through to what the jockey was wearing. Needless to say I couldn't remember any of it but suddenly my dad asked me what number the horse was and instantly I answered "number 6." What happened after that was enough to drive me insane because my dad went around telling everyone that number 6 was going to win the Grand National and explained his reason for assuming so. Everyone and their granny were then out placing bets on number 6 and I remember feeling that if this horse didn't come in first I would be burnt alive at a stake for being a witch. I myself put a tenner on it and like everyone else sweated in my result. Believe it or not the horse was the winner and a lot of people won money based on this weird dream and so I was saved from a horrific beating. Now that was the good luck because, as I mentioned, I placed a quick tenner on the said horse and should have netted quite a few quid but have a quick guess who lost their bookie docket and ended up totally skint?

Now the same luck was in when it came to romantic encounters. Me and a few friends some years ago founded an organisation known as the W.H.A.S. and although we started out with only two members we can now state that we have grown into quite a powerful organisation in terms of numbers, both male and female. Now before any Peelers reading this decide to investigate I should point out that the full title of our organisation is the Walk Home Alone Society because every time we went out on the touch that's exactly what happened. Now in fairness to our members it was never down to being ugly (except for one) but down to the simple fact that we never clicked on! A typical situation was being out in a bar or niteclub and being approached by a member of the opposite sex and chatted up. It was several hours later before one clicked on and that is the main criteria to being a member of the W.H.A.S. In case you're wondering why male and female members of the group never touch for each other the reason is quite simple - we never click on!

Reading the previous chapter then you'll know I love travelling but I will never stay more than three hours on a plane which limits me in terms of getting about. The first time I went to Moscow my dream was to see a statue known as the worker and the farmer but, as could be expected, everything was in Russian and it was a bit difficult to get about. You might think that there are better things in Moscow to see such as St Basil's and the Kremlin but to see these all we had to do was look out our hotel window. To put things into context this statue is my Knock as an old-school commie and is something that must be seen and touched. The worker is represented by a man holding a hammer and the farmer by a woman holding a sickle and when looked on from the sides the hammer and sickle cross to form the famous symbol we know today. The size of this statue is also beyond belief and before I had been to Moscow, I could describe it, tell you who designed it, who built it and even that Stalin changed the woman's head seven times. Unfortunately I've never even seen the thing and once again this is down to my out and out unfortunate luck.

If I go to the Russian capital tomorrow I could bring you to any part of the city using the Metro system but take my word for it that this was certainly not always the case. The first time I went I had it set in my head that this statue was the one thing I was not going to miss but have a quick guess what I did not see? The bottom line was I assumed Moscow would be the same size as somewhere like London but the fact of the matter was that a city such as Belfast would be described over there as a district - it is bloody big! Because of this I never got to see the statue because there were quite a few commie type parades on and these had to be watched, after all the statue was not going anywhere! Next time I went I was going to see this statue and absolutely nothing was going to stop me. Needless to say there were countless commie parades as well as the main military commemoration to mark the end of the Second World War and which comes complete with all the hallmarks of the Soviet regime. None-the-less I was not going to be distracted as this time I wanted to see this gigantic statue and nothing was going to stop me. Well that's where my luck kicks in!

After studying countless maps and Google Earth satalite pictures I worked out exactly where this statue was and found that it was not all that far from the hotel we were staying in - well a few miles! Because it was a beautiful day we decided to walk and after a few hours came to the area where the statue was situated but could see no sign of it and it is so big it would stick out a bit. Now I know you're thinking ask someone but this is Russia and once they hear you speak English (or

American as they call it) they automatically assume you're from the CIA. Now this area was the former Exhibition of Soviet Achievements and there was lots to see including various space craft including the world's first space shuttle which was never used because it was too dangerous (guess they were right on that one!)

At one end of the park was the worlds biggest fair ground wheel and we decided to go up on this to look down and see where this statue was. Needless to say we went up it and I can assure you that once up the last thing on my mind was the whereabouts of this bloody statue! Bad idea and once down to earth we decided that the good old fashioned way of looking for it at ground level would be a better option. After a short time we found it and that's where my luck kicks in. It was away being restored!

A few years ago I arranged a group visit from the Ashton Centre to go to Amsterdam and to state that everything that could go wrong did go wrong would be an understatement. To start with we had great fun getting flights for sixteen people and once that was done and paid for we then discovered that there was nowhere to stay. Now I know your reading this and thinking that it would be impossible not to get somewhere to sleep in a city such as Amsterdam but take my word for it - it can happen. It was then that I came up with this great idea of staying outside Amsterdam and the only nearby places I knew were Rotterdam, The Hague and Haarlem and because the latter was closer we decided on there. So into Holland we fly, get to the airport's underground railway and on to the train to Haarlem (below). Everyone was on board, no luggage was lost, the sun was shinning and everything was going well. Unfortunately that's where the luck also ended.

Once we got there there was not one single taxi outside the station and so we had to drag our luggage to the hotel which fortunately was only about half a mile away. Once we got there the spot on the map was not where the hotel was situated as this was a building site so we dragged our luggage up and down the street looking for the hotel and it was nowhere to be found. Because it was paid for I immediately thought that we had been stroked and our stay was going to consist of a few railway station benches. We made our way back down to the spot marked on the map and back to the building site when one of our group noticed a sign stuck up which read "Dear Mr Baker from Northern Ireland." It then went on to tell us that major renovation work was going on at the hotel but that we were to go to a nearby pub and ask for someone who was to give us keys to an apartment block nearby. This seemed like KGB stuff but we followed the instructions, went to the bar and

met the said person who gave us keys and told us where we were staying. We got there and to describe it as a hotel would be laughable but it was certainly better than sleeping in the railway station. Because I had all the keys I decided to suss out the rooms first and take the best for myself and picked one which had a brilliant view of the cathedral - it was literally feet from my window but as I was soon to find out It was a choice which was to cost me dearly. That night we went out for a few drinks which led to another few and then a few more. We got back to the 'hotel' and fell into bed for a good nights sleep. Now the said cathedral had a massive bell tower and it was well used but have a guess what time the said bells began to ring at? Well let me put it this way - at six o'clock in the morning I thought my eardrums were going to burst with the bloody noise! For the next few days we travelled by train into Amsterdam and had quite a good time. Now my fun was centred around shopping and visiting markets but I hear other people were drinking a lot and taking some sort of funny cigarettes but at least everything was going to plan and surely things could not go wrong now. When it came to getting home we went to Amsterdam and put our luggage into the storage containers at the railway station and spent our last few hours picking up prezzis and souvenirs of our stay but take my word for it what was to happen in another few hours would mean the last things we would need were momentos of our stay as it was one trip we were never, ever going to forget.

We went to the railway station, collected our luggage and headed back to the airport. Once there I remember asking one of the group what time 17.15 was. She replied that it was quarter past five and it was then I realised we had a major problem and to give you a clue as to what that problem was I asked the question at five past five. A major panic set in and we ran like mad to the check in area but for anyone who has ever been to Schiphol Airport then you'll know how big it is and the chances of getting from one end of it to another in the time we had were totally zero. For those who were on this trip they are going to be reading this and blaming

this on me but please allow me to present my case. The time on the sheet did indeed say 17.15 but the first number was faded and I really thought it said 7.15 but needless to say that did not stop my education being questioned and indeed my parentage!

We now realised that we had missed the flight and we made our way to the EasyJet desk to see what could be done. I had imagined that we were going to have to spend a few days picking tulips to get the money for our return flight but fortunately they managed to get us on the next one which was the next day so we were now stuck with an extra night and because none of us had any money it was really looking like an night spent on a railway station bench. We went down to the luggage storage area, placed our cases in the cabinets and decided to stay with them. In other words the whole lot of us ended up staying in the storage area for the next fifteen hours and I can tell you now it was hell as all the blame was sort of put in my direction. Needless to say we spent the next number of hours having a sleepless night and when we eventually made our way to the plane I can tell you that we made sure we were there a few hours before the check in opened.

Everyone still doubted my parentage but we ended up getting onto the plane and I remember sitting on my seat and thinking that nothing could possibly go wrong now. How wrong I was!

The plane took off and everything was going fine. I, along with the rest of my former friends had finally got seats and were having a bit of a kip when suddenly there was an announcement. It stated that we were not going to Belfast but because there was a problem with the ABS a landing would have to be made at Prestwick Airport in Scotland. It was then that I made one of the biggest mistakes of my life. I called down one of the cabin crew and and told him that I knew nothing about aircraft nor cars but going by TV advertisements for various vehicles ABS was something to do with brakes. I asked him was this the case here and he stated that the problem was that the brakes were not working and that the reason for landing at Prestwick was something to do with the fact that they had the longest runway. In other words landing the plane was not going to be a problem - stopping it was!

I can now tell you that the next hour was the most terrifying in my whole life and I (sorry we) really thought that this was it, our time was up. The way we spent our final hour was actually quite strange and while the whole plane was in panic we actually sat and worked out what our last words were going to be. I can't tell you what mine were but those around me went for the traditional 'Such is Life" and "Ah Well" but my favourite must go to a very close mate of mine who picked up a few iffy items of dodgy visual material who

wanted his last words recorded as "I never did get to see those DVD's" Needless to say I really can't believe we were all laughing in (what we really thought) were our last moments but we were.

Some time later we reached Scotland and began our descent. Now for those who believed that we really thought we were going to be OK and we were really not facing instant death in an aircraft crash landing all they had to do was look out the windows on the left hand side of the plane and the lines of fire engines and ambulances at the side of the runway sort of snapped you out of it. Now I'm sure you've worked out that things went all right as I'm writing this and in terms of not being killed in a fireball you'd be right but our problems did not end there. It was a military airfield and when we came off the plane instead of counselling what we got was detention as we were forced to stay in one room and not move from it until our next plane arrived to bring us to Belfast. Needless to say we went along with this and a few hours later our plane arrived to take us home. I'm glad to say that everything went incident free from there - yeah right!

We got to Belfast. We got picked up at the airport and taken back to the Ashton Centre and from there we all made our way home. For me the last number of hours were hell. I missed the flight. I made everyone stay in an airport locker room. I got them a flight where everyone really thought they were going to die. But in the end at least we all got home. I decided to get a taxi to my house as I had no energy left and was really exhausted. I remember going up the pathway to my house thinking about the lovely bed and comfy pillows that awaited me as I had not slept properly in three days. I put my key in the door and have a wee guess what broke!

TO CONCLUDE

Looking through this publication the reader could be forgiven for asking what kind of person has this all made me today? To be honest that is a question that I myself could never answer because I simply don't know. What I do know is that throughout my whole life I have been a victim of rumour and gossip most of which was totally untrue. However some of it was true and not all of it good. Growing up the way I did I can understand how I became a bad apple but in my defence I can honestly claim that I have never been wicked or evil towards anyone or anything and deep down I know that I am a caring person. I care about people and if there is any way I can help those in distress then I will. The same can be said about animals. I love our fellow creatures and never, ever in my whole life have I ever been cruel towards any of them. There are those who think that people involved in groups such as the Animal Liberation Front are a bunch of lunatics but I think they are caring individuals and I can fully understand their actions although not always agree with them. Do I think that people wearing fur coats should have buckets of paint thrown over them then the answer is no I don't. What I do agree with is people approaching them and asking the wearer if that is the remains of dead animals on their back and expressing their disgust. Do I think that the same should be done to those wearing leather then no I don't. Leather is from cows and unfortunately for them they are part of the human food chain and leather is a by-product. I am well aware that animals are going to be killed to feed us but so long as it's carried out in the least cruel way possible then that's what needs to be worked on. I have seen how people have treated animals and that has ranged from cats being skinned alive after being dipped in boiling water for their fur right through to sheep being strapped up by one leg and having its throat cut as part of some stupid religious rite. In Moscow I have seen so-called performing bears jumping up and down on one spot much to the amusement of those watching. What they don't realise is that they are watching insanity resulting from years of abuse and then give money towards (what they think are) cute dancing bears.

Man is a horrible creature who is on the verge of destroying the planet on which we live and not only is he extremely cruel towards animals but also towards other humans. I have no need to explain how this as almost all of us watch the news, but sadly most of us choose to bury our heads in the sand. There is also

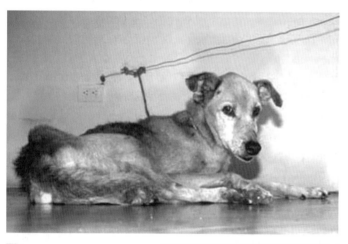

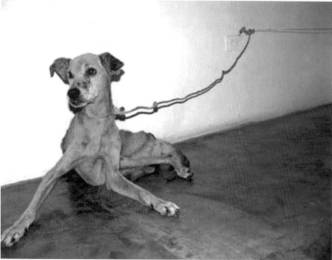

To give you an idea of the sort of cruelty which goes on this dog was taken of the streets, tied to a wire line and slowly starved to death. This was carried out as 'art' with visitors coming to watch this poor creatures misfortune

Thousands of children go missing each year and are sold into child slavery and the sex trade. Name one of them!

'selective caring' which is when people focus in on one tiny aspect of a much larger picture. For example look at the case of Madeleine McCann, the beautiful young child who went missing when on a family holiday in Portugal. Now don't pick me up wrong as the thought of your child being abducted and going missing is a nightmare for any parent but thousands of children go missing each year and are sold into slavery or the sex trade. My challenge to you would be to name one of them!

The other problem is that people think they are helpless to do anything and once again that is rubbish. In regards to animal cruelty there are those who think that this is carried out by some lunatic skinhead with his pitbull but you would be wrong. The skinheads with the pitbull are usually the ones who love their animals and the cruelty is generally carried out by those organising dog fights as part of betting scams attended by so called normal everyday people. Grass them up if you are suspicious of any of this. However the biggest form of animal cruelty is carried out by those conducting animal tests either for cosmetics or to advance medical science. Its all rubbish and for the proof all you have to do is look into it a little bit deeper. There is one case in which a rabbit has shampoo injected inside its eyeball but this begs the following question. What are the chances of you getting into the shower with your bottle of shampoo and accidentally injecting it inside your eyeball? As for medical advancements

then give a guinea pig penicillin and see what happens. To humans penicillin is a life saving drug but to a lot of animals it is deadly but once again what can you do? Don't buy products tested on animals nor be fooled by the labels which state that this product is not tested on animals. They are right as that product as a whole has not been tested on animals but what you should be looking for is this product and its ingredients have not been tested on animals. As for child slavery then once again do not think you are powerless. Those in the child slave trade are making well known brands for the western market - use the internet to find out which ones and simply don't buy them. As for the child sex trade ask yourself where the demand is coming from. Once again use the internet to find out where this is rife and question people you know about why they are going there and inform them of one of that countries tourist attractions - its as simple as that.

That's what I mean when I point out that I care about people and things and believe me the above is just a tiny sample. However I would also point out that I am no angel towards everyone. I've been in fights and burst peoples noses, knocked out teeth and when on to a looser bit them and bit them badly. There are former friends today whom I have not spoken a word to for years and one of these even includes my first wife. When I have been wronged I don't sit and plot how to get rid of them or work out revenge I just simply take nothing whatsoever to do with them. On the other hand there are people who I admire greatly and people who I detest and I don't even know them. Take J.K. Rowling who wrote all that Harry Potter stuff. She was a

J. K. Rowling

working class single mum who came from nothing and worked bloody hard to get where she is today. Then look at Paris Hilton and get me one person who would not love to get that spoilt *$%£@ and give her more than a good kick in the arse. You see what I mean!

It is also because of this that I am a communist and I have absolutely no shame in stating that nor, have I any shame with my hammer and sickle tattoos. There are those who state that communism has now fallen and no longer exists but take my word for it you're listening too much to the western news. We are led to believe that communism failed in the Soviet Union and therefore is a useless system but it did not fail as it was brought down by human greed and corruption. Most people in the former Soviet countries thought that they were going to be able to live in Coca-Cola paradise where their lives would be just like those portrayed in western television programmes. Sadly they now realise that it was all a bluff and now their quality of lives is far worse now that they have to pay for such things as rent, gas, electricity, health care and that there is no longer the guarantee of work. I have travelled to many former communist countries from East Germany, Czechoslovakia, Poland and Russia and hearing the stories of ordinary working class people is absolutely heart breaking.

Most are now living in poverty and hardship and all because they thought things were going to be so great on the other side - you know what they say about the grass being greener! I believe that communism is the best political system but I also fully acknowledge that it needs a touch of fine tuning and once a system can be worked out that can abolish greed and corruption then we are on to a winner. But there is another point that those who condemn it must remember. Recently we all witnessed the collapse of capitalism and it can be noted that it was the communist policy of nationalisation used to bail out the banks. I am well aware that there are those who are going to disagree but my challenge to them would be to justify why 2% of the population holds almost all the worlds wealth. Is that communist propaganda you may also ask. Nope - that's from the United Nations themselves!

Being a communist you would assume that my stance on religion would be that it is the 'superstition of the masses' but believe it or not it is actually far from it. Freemasons believe in 'The Great Architect of the Universe' regardless of this being from the Christian Bible, the Muslim Koran or Jewish Torah. They also believe that man's relationship with his God is a private matter. I would agree with them and while I don't practice any religion (nor am I a Freemason) I do believe that there is a higher being. I also believe that there is indeed a spirit within every human being. Another person I admire is Jesus because if you read his life story you'll see that in reality he was the world's first communist. He hated greed and corruption, defended the poor and when the boys ran out of drink turned water into wine!

You would also assume that I believe that everyone is equal but I don't. How can anyone state that a childcare worker is equal to a child molester? That a mass murderer is equal to a nun! What I do believe in strongly is that everyone should be given equal chances in life. I was brought up in a working class district and I will never allow anyone to look down his or her nose at me. To get where I am I have worked bloody hard and done a lot better than most spoilt brats with daddy's money and their private schools. I hate those who judge based on other peoples opinions. Have I judged people? Yes I have, but never on other peoples views. For example I have no hesitation in stating my hatred for those who exploit other peoples suffering for their own ends whether they be drug dealers or moneylenders. I have no hesitation in stating that I hate those who commit brutal cruelty towards helpless animals or humans.

Does this mean I am some sort of loony leftie politically correct type – believe me its far from it! I strongly believe that men and woman are equal but all this pc stuff sometimes does my head in when someone cannot be called a man or a woman but a person. My breaking point came quite a few years ago when I was at a seminar and was told of their support of a pending court case where a man was disciplined because he did not use the term 'personal access point' but instead called it a manhole. I walked out. To me a female, regardless of colour, religion, political belief or hairstyle is a woman. The same goes for a male whom I simply call a man. You would also be right in assuming I have very strong political opinions but have I ever sold out on my political beliefs – you're right I have. Quite a few years ago in Berlin there was a massive celebration to commemorate the founding of the European Union. Massive beer tents were erected in front of the Brandenburg Gate, stages were set up for live music and everything was set for a big party.

Naturally the spoil sports (i.e. – us) were there with our commie flags and banners to protest at the fact that the European Union was just an extension to the imperialist United States. As the protest was about to begin we found out that the live music was for everyone and the booze in the beer tents was completely free. Every protest banner and commie flag went straight into the bin and of to the tents we went!

I have no hesitation in admitting that I am a member of the Russian Communist Party and people may find that quite strange but there is a simple answer and that is in the fact that I plan to live there some day. Back in Ireland I once considered being a member of the Communist Party of Ireland but coming from the area I came from and the way I was brought up I guess I had to stick with the Erps.

Now I know there are going to be people from the Protestant/Unionist community who are going to call me a scumbag but take my word for it – I would help anyone from the loyalist community just as quickly as I would from the nationalist one. We are all aware of the changes in the politics of Northern Ireland over the past number of years and people are under the impression that these are for the better. Ok, granted, people are not killing each other any more and the bombings have stopped but what improvements do people think there will be? There are many of these developing and one of the first will be the eventual introduction of water charges. Like the vast number of people in Northern Ireland I will go with the flow because several like-minded people stood in the last elections against the water charges. Very few people voted for them so, going by democracy, that means the vast majority of people support the introduction of these extra bills!
Lets see how that works out!

Do I think there is going to be a United Ireland? Yes I do but this is going to be sneaked in gradually over a period of time. From the nationalist side the call had always been for a Federal Ireland. This changed to a Thirty Two County Socialist Republic and now this has changed to simply a New Ireland. We now have a Northern Ireland Parliament made up of nationalists and unionists with one thing to unite most of them them – massive wage packets!

This may appear that I am getting on my political platform here but take my word for it I am not. There are politicians out there I admire and these range from Sinn Fein right through to DUP. My belief today is that Ireland as a whole is simply the 51st state of the United States and a landing platform of NATO.

As for us in the North we are in the unique position where no one wants us. The Republic of Ireland don't want us and Britain can't wait to get rid of us.
Don't let me force this belief down your throat as this is just my opinion and, as far as Ireland is concerned, is simply a lost cause. My interest today is in people as individuals. More and more people are being exploited and this not only includes the obvious stuff but also includes people getting out high interest loans just so they could keep up with the Jones's. I am now more interested in helping out people as individuals and at the present time it is simply something I continue to do and which I can not write about.

I do it to this day and would encourage everyone else to do their part. It never needs to be anything big but if everyone done small parts think of the change it would make especially to the lives to those less fortunate. Look in on that old woman two doors down and ask her does she need anything in the shop. Change a light bulb for the disabled man in a wheelchair a few streets away and ask him if he needs anything else done. Kick a bit of broken glass to the side when walking up the street. Why chance some child falling on it and getting seven stitches across the face. Insignificant tiny acts can make a difference and this is the only way change will ever come about.

At the time of writing I am weeks away from my 45th birthday. In that time I have established my own successful publishing company and write for diverse Belfast newspapers. I am the chairman of one of the most successful community projects in both Ireland and Britain, which employs well over one hundred people. Because of extreme thirst I have drank holy water in the Vatican, looked into the face of Lenin and stood by the grave of Stalin as well as the first man in space Yuri Gagarin. Staying with space I patted the stuffed remains of Belka and Strecka the first two dogs in space, which returned to earth. I've nicked one of the tiles from the world's first space shuttle in Russia's Gorky Park. I have stood on the spot on which Adolf Hitler is said to have died and ate a meal while flying over the Alps. I have walked the streets of Troy and stood at the heart of the once mighty Roman Empire. I have stood in the Kremlin, the House of Lords and even shook hands with royalty (but did not bow),I have stood feet away from nuclear missiles and been kissed by a World War Two Soviet veteran. I proposed to my wife in Vienna, married her in Amsterdam and honeymooned in Moscow.
Not bad going for a New Lodge glue sniffer!

www.joebaker.ie

A BIG THANK YOU TOO ...

My Aunt Masie, Aunt Martha and Martin Lynch for material relating to my grandfather Robert Baker.

My cousin Robert Greer for information relating to mum's side of the family

My colleague Elaine Hogg for the first proof read.

A 'massive' thank you to Micky Liggett for the second proof read so any spelling mistakes blame these two!

Unknown photographers. Unfortunately I have no idea who owns some of the photographs used in the publication. If you think any may be yours please let me know so that I can acknowledge you in future reprints.

To Liam Baker not only for the cover photograph but also for doing what big brothers do over the years and who has remained my closest friend ever since.

Finally my wife Anne who had to put up with the lack of me while this was being written. To be honest I think she should be thanking me as she's the one who has to stick me 24/7

AND REMEMBER

This publication did not receive a single penny in funding and it is not intended to be for profit. All costs have been met by myself with the hope of helping out anyone who thinks for one minute that they are a failure to society. For many years it was my belief that I failed big time at school but it turned out that I did not fail the education system - the education system failed me! For those who find themselves in a similar situation remember what I have said - the only person holding you back is you!